OVERCOMING PANIC ATTACKS

OVERCOMING PANIC ATTACKS

Effective Strategies for Facing Anxiety and Taking Charge of Your Life

DAVID SHANLEY, PsyD

ROCKRIDGE
PRESS

Interior and Cover Designer: Brieanna Felschow
Art Producer: Karen Williams
Editors: Vanessa Ta and Samantha Holland
Production Manager: Martin Worthington
Production Editor: Sigi Nacson

Cover Illustration © Emmanuel Polanco 2020

Author photo courtesy of © John R Farrell Jr.

ISBN: Print 978-1-64611-724-6 | eBook 978-1-64611-725-3

R0

*To all my clients, who inspire me every day
with their courage to tackle their anxiety.
And to the love of my life, Kim.*

CONTENTS

INTRODUCTION

I have been in private practice for several years, specializing in working with adults with all forms of anxiety disorder, including panic disorder, obsessive compulsive disorder (OCD), social anxiety, post-traumatic stress disorder (PTSD), and more. In my work, I have witnessed that the common thread in all anxiety disorders, and specifically in those that involve recurring panic attacks, is the dreaded physical experience of panic and anxiety. The racing heart, the tightening chest, and the often indescribable, uncomfortable feeling throughout the body are all common to panic attacks. What seems to be the worst part about panic attacks is not always knowing where they are coming from because there's no obvious situational cue to point to as a cause and because their onset is so sudden.

Drawing from my personal experience, expertise, and clinical work with clients, in this book I unpack the mystery around panic attacks across many different life situations and offer you hope and tangible strategies to effectively deal with your panic attacks and reduce their frequency and severity. Although I would like to promise you a life free from anxiety and panic attacks moving forward, that outcome is neither realistic nor necessary for meaningful change. Instead, I offer you different ways of thinking, feeling, and behaving so that you will be able to increase your flexibility in uncomfortable situations and go after the life you want.

I've personally struggled with different forms of anxiety throughout my life. I have walked out of many interviews drenched in sweat, shied away from conversations at parties and networking events, and almost gotten sick when giving a speech at my best friend's wedding. Although I don't have panic disorder, I do know firsthand the negative, nagging inner voice that is screaming to avoid or escape a situation—the same voice undermining my confidence at the most inopportune times. The good news is by implementing the strategies discussed in this book, from exposure and cognitive reframing to mindfulness and acceptance, I have been able to overcome the grip anxiety had over my life, and you can, too. The strategies and tools discussed in this book come from cognitive behavioral therapy (CBT) and acceptance and commitment therapy (ACT).

CBT encompasses a wide array of interventions, including thinking about things in different ways, practicing and tracking new behaviors, and exposing yourself to uncomfortable and difficult situations in gradual steps. The benefits of CBT have been well researched and proven in hundreds of studies over several decades. The evidence is clear that these types of interventions can help people lower their anxiety in the long run and feel more confident in both challenging and everyday situations.

ACT is a newer form of behavioral therapy that shifts some of the emphasis from changing the content of thought patterns to noticing and accepting the process of thinking itself. It incorporates principles of mindfulness and acceptance to help people learn to tolerate and sit with discomfort rather than directly battle negative thoughts and feelings. ACT borrows ideas from Buddhism to teach us to be more patient and open to "negative" feelings, because in the end, to be human is to feel, and the struggle with our negative experiences is often a large part of what keeps us stuck. Ultimately, the goal of ACT is similar to CBT's, which is to increase flexibility in the presence of discomfort, thereby allowing people to have more energy to go after the life they want, like getting out in more social situations, giving speeches, traveling, interviewing for jobs, or just living without constantly trying to avoid and control panic.

How to Use This Book

This book offers several easy-to-implement strategies and techniques in each chapter for overcoming panic attacks across a broad range of situations and symptoms. All the strategies recommended here are either adopted from or closely related to techniques used in CBT and ACT. Both of these therapies are evidence based, meaning they have been scientifically tested numerous times to demonstrate their effectiveness. Although some of the strategies might be uncomfortable or scary at times, the more you practice, the more confident you'll become when using them. I won't ask you to do anything in this book I wouldn't do myself or wouldn't recommend to a close friend, family member, or client to help them with their panic and anxiety.

This book is presented in five chapters. In chapter 1, I'll discuss panic in general and how it differs from anxiety; you'll also have an opportunity to take a self-assessment to determine how panic attacks are affecting your life. You'll even have a chance to identify your values. Then, in chapters 2, 3, and 4, I'll walk you through different aspects of panic and share 12 to 14 strategies in each chapter for dealing with it in the body, in the mind (thoughts), and behaviorally (no more avoidance!). Chapter 5 reviews all the concepts discussed and offers ideas for taking your next steps. Feel free to jump around the chapters if some aren't speaking to you at the moment, but plan to return to them so that you can put all the strategies into practice. Getting overwhelmed and discouraged is often part of the journey toward progress, so I encourage you to put this book down and take breaks when you need to, but do come back to it. Always remember that panic, anxiety, and "negative" emotions are temporary and won't last forever.

Throughout, the Go Deeper sections offer suggestions on how to take the strategies to the next level by turning them into more in-depth exercises. I recommend that you use a notebook or a journal alongside this book, or, if you'd like, you can use your phone or other device to take notes or even record your responses to questions or prompts. Even if you don't do the additional work, you will still be able to implement many of the techniques in this book, so please do whatever works for you. The goal is for you to gain confidence and flexibility in the presence of panic and anxiety so you can get your life back. You may find that you must practice some of the same techniques multiple times before they start to click, whereas others may bring you some relief on the first or second try. Don't get discouraged—practicing is all part of your healing journey!

With all techniques and exercises, the more you practice, the better you get. We are creatures of habit, and if you picked up this book, your brain has likely spent many years strengthening certain pathways that may be counterproductive in dealing with panic. As such, it will take some repetition, patience, and willingness on your part to get comfortable and to retrain your brain to break the cycles of anxiety and panic. I recommend practicing strategies in both easier and more difficult situations so that when you need them most, they are second nature to you.

This book is designed for your personal use as well as for use in conjunction with therapy. It is not meant to replace professional help. If you are experiencing anxiety or panic symptoms that are negatively impacting your daily life and/or ever have suicidal thoughts, it's important to contact a therapist or psychiatrist. The National Suicide Prevention Lifeline is available 24 hours a day: 1-800-273-8255.

Chapter 1

Is Panic Running Your Life?

You've probably heard people say that they "panicked" in a certain situation, but there is a definite distinction between your experience and the momentary fright someone without panic disorder might feel in a threatening situation. A person without the disorder can still experience the classic symptoms of panic and anxiety that can compel them to take action in an emergency, but panic attacks are not a regular occurrence in their life. In this chapter, I'll discuss what panic disorder is and the typical symptoms associated with it as well as how it differs from anxiety. At the end of the chapter, you can do a self-assessment to determine how panic is impacting your everyday life and identify the values that are important to you. I encourage you to be honest with yourself, as acceptance of the situation is the only way to begin to heal.

When Panic Strikes

Panic disorder is an anxiety disorder in which a person struggles with recurring, unexpected panic attacks. It also includes the fear of having panic attacks, usually in places or situations where it may be inconvenient to have one because escape is difficult and/or public embarrassment is likely.

Classic physiological symptoms of a panic attack, many of which you have likely experienced, include a racing heart, tightening in the chest, sweating, changes in breathing patterns (possibly hyper-ventilating), redness in the face, tingling in the hands and feet, chills, dizziness, nausea, feeling like you are choking, trembling, and shaking. Thoughts that you are going to die or have a heart attack, feeling like you are going crazy, or thinking the panic attack will never pass are some common cognitive symptoms of the disorder. Emotionally, you may feel frightened, anxious, overwhelmed, filled with dread, and as if you are losing or out of control. Occasionally, you may experience derealization or depersonalization—the feeling that either you are not real or the situation or surrounding is not real, momentarily skewing your perception of reality.

Panic attacks can occur seemingly out of nowhere and can happen anywhere, but some common places you might struggle with the dis-order include airplanes, highways, shopping malls, sporting events, open spaces, bridges, confined places, concerts, schools, grocery stores, meetings, social events, and even at home. You might start to become so frustrated by the unpredictability of panic attacks that you fear leaving your home entirely. But being a shut-in is not the answer; your life would only become narrower and more isolated, leading to further anxiety and possibly depression.

Avoidance behaviors often accompany panic disorder as an instinc-tual way of coping with fear. These attempts to mitigate, escape, or avoid panic attacks include leaving a situation, staying home or isolated, or using substances to dampen panic feelings. When you start predicting the situations that cue up your panic, it makes it easier for you to avoid those specific situations where the panic attack is more likely. For instance, if you anticipate having a panic attack on an airplane, you might still be able to go to work, hang out with friends, or go to the grocery store without affecting the number of panic attacks you experience because you are not spending time in the panic-inducing situation. However, if the situations that cause panic attacks are ones that are important to you (for example, taking a flight to visit your family), then the avoidance of these situations can have a significant (and potentially negative) impact on your life.

Although anyone can experience panic attacks, people who have been exposed to traumatic events, combat zones, or other near-death experiences often report feelings of panic in crowded or unknown environments. These panic attacks are part of post-traumatic stress disorder (PTSD), another form of anxiety disorder that has similar symptoms to panic disorder. For good reason, people with PTSD have learned to distrust the world or strangers and have a heightened sensitivity to the dangers of the world. It is evolutionarily advantageous that humans are very fast learners when it comes to dangers and threats. When one has been exposed to these dangers, there is no "unlearning" that can take place to help them forget to be vigilant. However, not all hope is lost if this is the case for you. Learning techniques and strategies and developing new behaviors can gradually help you become more comfortable in challenging environments.

Living in a near-constant state of panic or having recurring panic attacks may lead to additional consequences. Our bodies are impacted by panic attacks, too. On the physiological side, people who suffer from panic attacks are more prone to gastrointestinal distress, including constipation or diarrhea. They might also experience temporary spikes in blood pressure during panic episodes. Although these symptoms are unlikely to cause long-term problems, it is always important to let your doctor know what you have been experiencing. Similarly, there is some research identifying a link between panic attacks and asthma. It seems asthma and other respiratory problems can be made worse by panic attacks, and it is natural for someone to develop a fear of having another panic attack if they experienced difficulty breathing during the last one. A health care practitioner can help you reduce the impact of these problems.

Panic versus Anxiety

Although panic and anxiety are often talked about interchangeably, there are a few key distinctions between the two. First, to be classified as panic, the physiological symptoms must be present. Panic always involves the intense, acute rush of adrenaline and associated physical feelings experienced throughout the body. These symptoms are typically the most dreaded part of the panic attack, as they are so difficult to control, especially in the moment. The *Diagnostic and Statistical Manual of Mental Disorders* (5th edition), the go-to source for diagnosing mental health issues, defines a panic attack as the presence of at least four of the symptoms mentioned earlier (see When Panic Strikes, page 2).

One key component of panic disorder versus other forms of anxiety is the duration of the experience. Most panic attacks last at peak intensity for approximately 15 to 30 minutes, sometimes less (depending on a variety of factors). Although the experience is heart-pounding and gut-wrenching, the actual duration is relatively short. After that peak-intensity period, you'll usually notice a "coming down," or calming effect, as your body comes back to rest. Rest assured that your body will not keep you in a state of panic for hours on end; instead, the parasympathetic nervous system will kick in to protect your body.

On the other hand, those who struggle with other forms of anxiety might ruminate for hours, days, or weeks and feel a sense of dread without experiencing the intense physiological symptoms associated with panic. They may worry about a specific looming event or something that didn't go well in the past. Their thoughts may involve the details of worst-case scenarios or an endless stream of "what ifs?" as well as many moments of self-doubt and inadequacy.

During a panic attack, anxiety-provoking thoughts are magnified and seem catastrophic. When your body is charged up during a panic attack, your mind can create stories to match the experience. For example, if your heart is racing uncontrollably, it might feel like the stress on your heart is going to lead to a heart attack. Similarly, numbness or tingling in your arm mimics the symptoms of a heart attack, and your mind very quickly fills in the gaps to assume you must be having one.

Heart attacks are one of the leading causes of death in the United States, so it's logical for our minds to infer that death could be imminent in the midst of a panic attack. This assumption can lead to multiple unnecessary and expensive trips to the emergency room. Panic attacks do not, and will not, actually cause a heart attack in the moment. However, some studies indicate that panic disorder, if left untreated, is associated with an increased risk of developing heart disease over time. Therefore, it is important to learn how to minimize the impact of panic attacks. If you do have cardiac issues or are unsure about your overall health, see your doctor for a routine visit and get everything checked out. If you have done so and been told that you seem healthy and your heart and blood pressure are fine, I want you to start thinking about these panic attacks for what they are—fleeting, terrifying experiences that will most certainly pass.

Predictable versus Unpredictable Attacks

A key distinction between panic disorder and other anxiety disorders is the idea of cues—a logical or coherent path that can be followed to find the source. An obvious cue can make some other forms of anxiety more predictable. For example, if you were in a car accident on the highway, it makes sense that you would feel some anxiety about driving on the highway in the future. Your mind learned that highway driving is "dangerous" or "threatening" from that experience, so now you avoid highways. Because your mind has not had the opportunity to experience safely driving on the highway since the accident, your avoidance of the situation maintains the anxiety around highway driving.

With panic attacks, however, it is trickier. One panic attack might occur at the grocery store, the next at a social event, and another at work, without any common trigger that you can detect. In other words, there's no obvious cue and it seems unpredictable. Not knowing how or when a panic attack is going to happen makes living with panic disorder feel even more frightening. We all want assurance and predictability, and we fear uncertainty. It's the way mammals, including humans, are wired. Various studies have demonstrated the physiological stress response to unpredictability. In one study at Kurume University School of Medicine in Japan, scientists determined that uncertainty and the consequent feeling of being out of control were so aversive to rats that they showed physiological distress and, as a result, did whatever they could to get away. Who could find fault with the rats' behavior?

Panic attacks are so alarming because they seem to lack predictability and certainty about what is happening, how long it will last, and what the consequences will be. You are not crazy for feeling scared, upset, and anxious about this uncertainty. Anyone would feel that way. Life is hard enough as it is. You may be trying to balance work, friends, social life, rent or mortgage, car payments, health concerns, and a myriad of other responsibilities. On top of all of that, a panic attack could hit at any given moment. That's why you are reading this book and looking for information and strategies to make the experience more manageable.

As you work through this book (and/or work with a therapist), you may notice that although your panic attacks seem unpredictable, there are usually hidden cues. As the saying goes, "The devil is in the details." It is therefore your job moving forward to start gathering data on your panic attacks to better understand them and see if there is a pattern to those distressing experiences. These cues could involve something less obvious, such as worrying about the health of a loved one; feeling trapped in a dead-end job, career, or relationship; or being concerned about your health, happiness, or mortality, to name just a few examples. Your worries may be incredibly valid, but that knowledge doesn't make the panic attack go away.

You will need to figure out if your panic attacks are cued, or can be predicted, by something you can identify or not. The more information you find out about yourself, the faster you will learn how to deal with your panic. Keep in mind that there may be no rhyme or reason for the panic attack that you can identify, and that's perfectly okay, too. Even if you never know why you have panic attacks, you can still learn to reduce their severity and frequency.

Fear of Panic

Cues for panic attacks are often subtle or seemingly impossible to identify. Suddenly everything can start to feel like a possible cue or situation for a panic attack. The original panic attack might have had a more "legitimate" cause, such as being stuck somewhere or feeling embarrassed about being in the spotlight. Maybe it started with some physiological symptoms, like profuse sweating and shaking, and then spiraled into catastrophic thoughts (like you were in the midst of a nervous breakdown) quite quickly, thus taking you out of the moment and making it harder to focus on performing a task, carry on a conversation, or drive on the highway. The fear of having another panic attack can be firmly established after just one experience.

Depending on your first experience of a panic attack, the feeling of being out of control and the acute physiological symptoms might have been incredibly intense, and anything that might remotely remind you of the situation where you had the first attack becomes associated with the fear of having another attack. Our minds are hardwired to learn and remember dangers incredibly quickly and efficiently. And thanks to books, movies, and television, we can think about, imagine, and cue up dangers and associations between situations and events without even experiencing them firsthand!

The complexity of the brain is a double-edged sword when it comes to anxiety and panic. It works so well to keep us safe from danger but can also keep us paralyzed by fear, even when there is no real danger present. The path of panic disorder can be a seemingly endless cycle of fear where you want nothing more than to not experience another panic attack. You start looking for ways to keep yourself safe from panic, avoiding what you think must be triggering it. You may even try to convince yourself that you don't really care about traveling, camping, socializing, going to crowded places, experiencing the world, and so on.

As you will learn throughout this book, attempts at avoiding and controlling panic attacks often make them worse. Remember, you must come to an understanding that there may be no rhyme or reason you can identify for the panic attack, and that it does not mean that you are actually going crazy, having a heart attack, or going to die. It just means that you might need to learn other strategies to manage panic attacks more effectively in the moment so that they do not start to dictate your life. I can tell you firsthand from working with dozens of clients suffering from panic attacks and panic disorder that the road is not always clear and straightforward, but there *is* a path to relief from suffering and to regaining control over your life. By practicing the strategies in this book, the path to relief will become clearer.

How Is Panic Affecting Your Life?

You've probably been trying to avoid the panic that has negatively impacted your life in some manner. However, panic disorder affects people in different ways. It is time to take honest stock of how panic is impacting your life. This book will provide a road map to the areas you need to focus your goals on most. You will become more aware of the extent of the problem, which will motivate you to take steps to find relief. Finally, the act of acknowledging the extent of your panic is a great first step to exposure to and acceptance of uncomfortable thoughts and feelings. Start looking at where panic might appear in your daily life and activities by asking yourself the following questions, and then you'll have an opportunity to complete a self-assessment.

Do your panic attacks occur during everyday moments, chores, activities, and tasks, such as going to grocery stores, restaurants, shopping malls, or other crowded spaces? Do you fear having a panic attack while driving, flying, camping, or traveling? Although some of these activities are optional, it is important to assess how much you are letting panic control your life. If you don't want to do something as extreme as skydiving to avoid a panic attack, it would have little to no effect on the rest of your life. But not doing something ordinary, like going to the grocery store, to avoid panic attacks is functionally different and gives the panic too much power. I understand how hard and scary panic attacks are to deal with, but I really want to drive home the message that you can take back control of your life—*you* get to decide what to do with your behavior, whether or not panic shows up.

Does panic arise when you are meeting up with friends, family, strangers, acquaintances, or a date? Do you struggle more when you are going to a party or an event where you will be expected to "just socialize and talk" rather than if there is some sort of planned activity (such as a family gathering, concert, sporting event, game night, bowling, movie, etc.)? Is there a sense of dread leading up to the event or a burst of panic in the last few minutes right before going into a situation? Has panic led you to isolate yourself or to refuse to engage in relationships in the first place?

Many people with panic disorder fear that others will reject them because of their anxiety and panic, and that panic is preventing them from having healthy relationships, so they avoid them altogether, which can lead to severe consequences of isolation, loneliness, and depression. It doesn't have to be this way. Humans are relational beings—we need relationships and social contact to survive and thrive. Believe it or not, almost everyone has had some experience of anxiety, and possibly panic, at some point in their lives, so they are actually very unlikely to reject you for it.

Do your panic attacks happen at your workplace, perhaps when you are asked to handle unfamiliar work-related duties or if you have to attend a meeting, ask your boss for something, work on a team, or do something in an unfamiliar setting? Is fear of having a panic attack at an inopportune time at your job leading you to avoid certain tasks or situations, resulting in missed opportunities, feelings of hopelessness and worthlessness, or a sense of being stuck when you know deep down that you are capable of or interested in pursuing a desired position, role, or project?

Avoidance can apply to more than just places or situations that you physically avoid. Panic attacks can start trapping you in a mindset that makes you feel like you must always have certain safety parameters in place in order to engage in different situations. For example, it is common for someone with panic disorder to develop the habit of never leaving the house without their antianxiety medication. Similarly, they might decide they can no longer go out without being accompanied by someone they trust in fear of having a panic attack alone. Although I certainly encourage turning to friends and family for support, it is critical to give yourself the opportunity to develop trust and confidence in yourself by not avoiding taking on challenges alone.

Is the fear of having a panic attack causing you ongoing misery and distress? If so, it's time to tackle your panic attacks head-on and regain control over your life!

Panic Self-Assessment

This self-assessment is divided into three sections: physiological symptoms, cognitive symptoms, and avoidance behaviors. For the symptoms you know you're afraid of or tend to experience, either check them off here or write them in your notebook or device. Put a star next to any symptom that is especially troublesome or causes you the most distress. After you go through the list, in your notebook or device, jot down where you tend to experience it (for example, social events, school, work, crowds, home, driving, confined spaces, open spaces, etc.).

Physiological Symptoms

Which of the following physiological symptoms do you experience during a panic attack and/or worry about experiencing?

- Shallow breathing
- Tightening of chest
- Choking sensations
- Coldness/chills
- Gastrointestinal issues
- Rapid heart rate
- Hot flashes
- Hyperventilating

- Lightheadedness/dizziness
- Nausea
- Stomach pains
- Sweating
- Tingling/numbness
- Trembling/shaking
- Tunnel vision
- Something else?

Cognitive Symptoms

Which of the following thoughts have you experienced during a panic attack and/or worry about experiencing?

- *I'm going to die.*
- *I'm having a heart attack.*
- *I can't handle this.*
- *I'm losing control.*
- *I'm losing my mind.*

- *What if I never calm down?*
- *I feel trapped.*
- *I can't tell what feels real.*
- *I need to get out of my body.*
- Other thoughts?

Avoidance Behaviors

Which of the following places, situations, or things do you avoid because you fear you will have a panic attack?

- Airplanes
- Alcohol
- Bridges
- Caffeine
- Class/school
- Close friendships
- Crowded spaces/big public events
- Elevators
- Grocery stores
- Gyms

- Highways
- Job interviews
- Meetings
- Networking events
- Public speaking
- Presentations
- Romantic relationships
- Social events
- Travel
- Something else?

Which safety behaviors do you use to avoid panic attacks or to prepare yourself in case you might have one?

- Always carry a bottle of water with you

- Always carry a certain medication with you

- Avoid places at certain times of day

- Avoid going out of the house alone

- Avoid going to places/events when you feel "off" or are not in the "right mindset"

- Something else?

Now that you have a clearer picture of what your panic disorder looks like, you will have a better idea of how the strategies discussed in the upcoming chapters will be useful while you are trying to engage more fully in your life and live in alignment with your values.

What Do You Value?

Knowing what your values are is probably the most important part of the work you'll be doing. Values are how we clarify what is important to us, what we want our lives to be about, how we want to be in the world and with others, and how we want to prioritize areas of our lives. Health could be a value, as could family, career, education, or personal recreation or leisure. Another value could be laughter, kindness, honesty, integrity, or compassion, as a way of being with others and interacting in the world. There are no right or wrong values. The whole idea is that values are yours to choose, and they should resonate with you on a deep, meaningful level. Your values aren't something you think your parents, significant other, boss, or someone else wants you to have. Values are yours. They are also not goals. They are more like compass headings for directions to take your life. You can work toward your values for the rest of your life without ever "finishing them," so to speak. Health and kindness are not things you accomplish and then check off the list. They are things you continue to orient your life toward.

Values are important because they don't change based on thoughts and feelings. Whether or not you're having a panic attack, you still have your values. To start clarifying your values, reflect on these questions:

- What kind of life do you want?

- What kind of relationships do you want?

- How important is your job or career?

- What activities do you want to be engaged in?

- If panic attacks, anxiety, or other stressors were no longer a problem, what would you do with your life?

>

- What qualities do you value in yourself?

- What kind of person do you want to be in this world?

- How do you want to be with/toward others?

- How important are health and well-being to you?

Take some time to expand upon each area of your life that you identified as being part of your values. For example, if career is a value of yours, is it a salary, particular kind of job, or setting that is important to you? Don't worry right now about filtering your responses, even if you recognize that you may not be going after everything you identified as being important to you. Keeping your values in mind can provide you with the motivation to do the work in this book.

TAKEAWAYS

- Panic attacks involve relatively short, scary, intense, and acute physiological symptoms of fear. With effort and practice, you can gain control over how you deal with them.

- Panic attacks can be unpredictable, often making them scarier and keeping you stuck in a cycle of fearing when or where the next panic attack may occur.

- Be honest with yourself about how panic attacks are affecting different aspects of your life. You need to become an expert on your experience of panic attacks as a first step toward dealing with them.

- Defining your values provides you with motivation to go after the life you want and deserve.

Chapter 2

Your Body and Physiological Signs of Panic

The physiological symptoms of a panic attack are extremely distressing. So, in this chapter, we'll dive further into the details about what is going on in the body during a panic attack and what you can do about it. The CBT- and ACT-based strategies and exercises in this chapter can help you get to know your body and its processes better as well as help you engage in behaviors aimed at generally lowering your anxiety levels. No single strategy will entirely eliminate your anxiety and panic, of course. That result is just not realistic. Instead, the best perspective is one of openness, curiosity, courage, flexibility, and willingness. This attitude is consistent with the ACT philosophy of approaching and accepting discomfort, staying present, and noticing your experience without judgment. I want you to be less caught up in judgments about what is happening and become more in touch with seeing these experiences for what they are: passing sensations.

Panic and the Body

Just before a panic attack, the amygdala (sometimes called the brain's alarm) perceives a threat, and the sympathetic nervous system (one of the two main divisions of the autonomic nervous system) is activated. Adrenaline, cortisol, and other stress hormones are released, leading to increased blood flow in the parts of the body that need it most to either fight off a threat or escape it as quickly as possible. This reaction is what is known as the fight-or-flight response.

During the fight-or-flight response, the heart pumps blood quickly through your large muscle groups (the legs, arms, and shoulders). Your breathing quickens, your vision narrows, and your body temperature rises, causing sweating. These symptoms are evolutionarily adaptive physiological responses designed to help us physically handle a threat. At the same time, attention is drawn away from nonessential systems in the body, which are controlled by the parasympathetic nervous system (the other main division of the autonomic nervous system), such as digestion, sometimes leading to nausea or the feeling that your stomach is "in knots."

It's actually quite amazing how effective this system is at responding so efficiently and automatically when a threat is perceived. This response is especially helpful when a real threat is present, such as a lion running toward you. However, the system is also activated when a threat is just perceived or thought about, as is often the case in a panic attack. The mechanisms at play respond very quickly without your having to think about what is going on. The faster the system kicks in, the more effective it is at keeping us safe. The downside is that it is very hard to just "turn off" the system once it's been activated. If you've ever heard a car backfire or been startled by someone who walked up behind you, you've likely felt an immediate rush of adrenaline. Your body responded before you even had a chance to think, *Was that a car backfiring or a gunshot?* or *Is that a friend behind me, or is someone trying to hurt me?*

The stress hormones that are released during the fight-or-flight response are useful in the moment, but they can have damaging effects if they stay in the system for extended periods. Some of the long-term symptoms of stress are gastrointestinal problems, irritable bowel syndrome (IBS), high blood pressure, and sleep disruption. To minimize these effects, it is important for everyone to learn ways to cope with and manage their stress more effectively.

Following the fight-or-flight response, the parasympathetic nervous system steps in to begin the process of coming down. Calming hormones, such as acetylcholine, are released; muscles are relaxed; vision returns to normal; and nonessential functions are restored. You might feel a sense of relief, exhaustion, coldness, or relaxation as your body resets itself after a panic attack. This process can take anywhere from 20 to 60 minutes, depending on the person and severity of the attack.

Panic attacks can feel like a full body and brain workout. It is completely understandable if, after experiencing a panic attack, you are tired for the rest of the day, are not as productive at work, or want to stay home for the night instead of going out. It is perfectly fine to take care of yourself and nurture yourself after a panic attack. You are allowed to take a break and put yourself (and your health) first. If, on the other hand, you had a panic attack in the morning and cancel plans later that evening because you fear having another panic attack, you are not nurturing yourself; that behavior is avoidance. Avoidance is a key process I will come back to throughout this book to help you develop the strength, courage, and coping tools necessary to engage fully with your life.

WHERE DOES MY PANIC SHOW UP?

As with many challenges in life, the best way to overcome an obstacle is to get to know it inside and out. As such, one great strategy is to learn how panic shows up in your body. You won't become an expert overnight, but becoming aware of the nuances is a good first step.

This exercise may be uncomfortable, but take a moment now to think about your panic attacks in general. You can eventually work up to asking yourself these questions during an actual panic attack, but don't force it. This ACT strategy helps you increase your present-moment awareness of your body's physical experience during a panic attack. It is a key component of approaching, accepting, and disarming the discomfort associated with panic attacks.

- Where in your body does the panic usually show up? Try to pinpoint specific areas.

- What sensations do you notice? Numbing? Tingling? Tension? Heat? Chills? What else?

- Do you sweat? Feel nauseous? Dizzy? Lightheaded? What else?

By acknowledging what happens in your body during a panic attack, you are one step closer to knowing what to do about it, and you are teaching your brain that you can think about, face, and manage these distressing experiences.

BODY SCAN

A body scan is a mindfulness strategy aimed at better connecting with your body. Consistent with the ACT principles of mindfulness, acceptance, and nonjudgmental awareness, this experience also teaches you to be present and grounded, which will help give you a sense of control during a panic attack. Start by practicing the body scan when you are feeling relaxed. Go somewhere you won't be disturbed for at least a few minutes, and get comfortable. You can do the scan either sitting or lying down.

Once you are comfortable, breathe normally and begin to mindfully (meaning slowly and intentionally, without judging sensations as good or bad) "scan" your body from head to toe. Start with your head, and slowly work your way down through the different muscle groups and parts of your body: your face, neck, chest, shoulders, arms, hands, abdomen, buttocks, thighs, calves, and feet. Notice any tension or discomfort as well as a sense of relaxation, again without judgment. Just notice.

Try this exercise when you are feeling calm and also when you are feeling revved up but not panicked so you can notice the different sensations. The more you practice the body scan, the better you will become at simply noticing what's going on in your body without judging it. This technique can eventually come in handy during a panic attack to help you regain a sense of control.

CHECK YOUR PULSE

A common fear many have during a panic attack is that their heart is going to beat so fast that a heart attack, or possibly death, is imminent. Although I understand that it feels like a real possibility in the moment, it will not happen. To get a handle on these thoughts and feelings, start to become familiar with your heart rate, beginning with your resting heart rate. According to the Mayo Clinic, a normal resting heart rate for adults ranges from 60 to 100 beats per minute.

To find your resting heart rate, check your pulse while you are relaxing. Using your middle finger and index finger, find your pulse on your opposite wrist below the thumb side of your hand. Now, set a timer for 10 seconds, and count the number of beats you feel during the 10 seconds. Multiply this number by six. This number is your resting heart rate.

You can also measure your heart rate during and after various types of physical activity to get an idea of how your heart rate fluctuates. It's almost like you are a scientist observing a fascinating function of your body. Check your pulse from time to time to become comfortable with the idea of measuring your heart rate during and after a panic attack. Becoming familiar with how your heart rate normally fluctuates can help put your mind at ease in the moment, allowing you to practice accepting your quickened heart rate for what it is.

TAKE YOUR PANIC ATTACK FOR A WALK

Wait, what? That's right! The next time you feel like a panic attack might be coming on, a good strategy to practice acceptance of your symptoms is to get up, move around, and go for a walk. Walking has many benefits, including expelling energy, getting fresh air, grounding yourself, and putting control back in your own hands. Note the wording here: *You* are in control and taking your panic attack along for a walk. *You* make the decisions and control your behavior, not your panic. Your panic symptoms are going to come and go as they please, and this exercise in acceptance of your body and what is happening will ultimately reduce your fear of the whole experience. This spin on a classic ACT strategy promotes acceptance and committed action in the face of discomfort. I know facing panic is hard, and this exercise will help you gain confidence.

Go Deeper: Really Get to Know Your Panic Experience

I know this idea probably sounds terrible, but as I mentioned earlier (and will get into more later), there is tremendous benefit to leaning into the panic—letting yourself feel the experience rather than escaping and avoiding it. Noticing and embracing the sensations will have a disarming effect on them, teaching you through your direct experience that you can handle the feelings and symptoms, as unpleasant as they are. Part of leaning into a panic attack involves becoming curious about it. This exercise makes you a scientific observer of your own panic, so you can see what exactly happens to your body during an episode. The benefit is that it will give you something to focus on other than alarming thoughts and will give you a sense of accomplishment and control. It's okay if it takes you a while to build up to doing this exercise during a panic attack. Practice when you are feeling relaxed and after some physical activity so it feels more natural to try it during a panic attack.

In the strategy on page 23, you learned how to measure your heart rate. You can also measure your respiratory rate (the number of breaths per minute). While you are resting, set a timer for 20 seconds, and count how many breaths you were able to complete in that time. Multiply that number by three to get your number of breaths per minute. The average respiratory rate for an adult at rest is 12 to 20 breaths per minute. You can also try it after physical activity to see how your respiratory rate fluctuates. It doesn't matter if your breaths are long and deep or fast and shallow. The goal is not to judge; the goal is just to get to know what's really happening. Maybe you always assumed you were hyperventilating during a panic attack. This exercise will give you concrete data instead of relying on your not-so-trustworthy mind.

Another step to take is to check where you are sweating. Is there noticeable sweat on your hands, armpits, chest, forehead, back, or somewhere else? Simply make a mental note of the areas, as there is nothing you need to do about it. Your body is regulating its temperature, which requires no additional intervention from you. It's just nice information to have to better evaluate your panic attacks. You can practice during an ordinary day when you've exerted some effort and break a sweat to help you get comfortable noticing this type of information during a panic attack.

Also take note of any body parts that are tingling. Maybe you are experiencing this sensation in your toes, feet, hands, arms, or stomach. When you notice an area, simply say to yourself, "Tingling in left arm," or whatever body part is experiencing something. Practicing the body scan discussed in the strategy on page 22 can help you become more familiar with physical sensations in everyday moments to make identifying them during an attack a little easier.

In your notebook or device, jot down the "data" you collect during rest, during activity, and during a panic attack, and track your responses over time. Also, write about your experience of what it was like to be an observer of these measurements and sensations. Was it difficult, easy, scary, boring, and/or interesting?

The Mind–Body Connection

An important principle in both ACT and CBT is to take active steps to promote a healthy lifestyle. There are a few key aspects of our physical health we have control over that can make a huge difference in anxiety, panic, and mood. They are the common things you hear doctors and friends give you advice about all the time because they actually are important and make a difference in daily life. I'm talking about proper sleep, physical activity, and nutrition.

When you take care of these aspects of your life, you will feel less stressed and more energized in general, so that when panic does hit, you will be in a better position to handle the symptoms, which may also peak at a lower level. You may also find that panic attacks are occurring less frequently. But because panic attacks and the fear of having them can disrupt your ability to get proper sleep, your motivation to engage in physical activity, and the effort it takes to eat nutritious foods, it is important to be compassionate with yourself and committed to making healthy choices, even when your mind tells you that you can't.

Sleep

New research is always coming out about the importance and benefits of regular sleep. As you've likely experienced, when you don't sleep well, you don't feel well. You might feel cranky, groggy, foggy, depressed, or anxious, and it could have absolutely nothing to do with situational or emotional factors and everything to do with sleep. Sleep is where we rest and recharge, and give all of the systems in the body a chance to reset and get ready for the challenges of the next day. If you're not sleeping well, it could also affect your appetite and energy levels as well as exercise, work, or social activity—all of which can have further consequences. Furthermore, a lack of sleep can lead to feeling "off," jittery, or unsettled, which could possibly trigger a panic attack. A panic attack that occurs at night can make it difficult to wind down or fall asleep, especially if your mind is racing. Taking care of your sleep and yourself is part of building healthy habits that can give you the energy to face and endure panic attacks and perhaps make them less intense.

Physical Activity

Engaging in physical activity is an important area of life that so often gets neglected when we get stressed, depressed, or anxious, but it is actually one of the best antidotes for anxiety and panic. However, exercise can mimic some of the physiological symptoms of panic (such as increased heart rate, shallow breathing, and sweating), which may, understandably, alarm you. If certain exercises cause your anxiety to spike in the short term, know that physical activity can be as simple as taking a walk or gardening. And although exercise can be a triggering activity for some people with panic attacks, it is also a great opportunity for exposure and cognitive restructuring, which you'll learn about in upcoming chapters. Getting to know your body and its limits while building tolerance for uncomfortable sensations is one of the goals of this work.

In general, moving your body gets the "feel-good" endorphins firing in your brain, boosting confidence and self-esteem, and it also provides an opportunity to physically work out some of the nervous energy that can build up from the pressures of everyday life. The increase in self-confidence can help you feel more positive in general with regard to dealing with your panic attacks. There are so many benefits to physical activity and zero drawbacks (as long as you are doing things that are within your physical abilities).

Nutrition

Good nutrition is essential to mental health because the brain relies on a variety of nutrients to function. Of course you want your brain to work well, but when you are dealing with panic and anxiety, it might be difficult to make the best choices. You may find yourself turning to comfort foods or fast foods to make yourself feel better. However, eating candy, chips, cake, and other high-carb junk food can cause spikes and crashes in your blood sugar levels, which can potentially exacerbate your anxiety. Your mind will try to make sense of signals in the body, including low energy, energy spikes, blood sugar crashes, nausea, and stomach pains, and it may interpret one or more of the signals as the onset of a panic attack. Although I understand the draw to consume these foods, you will be better off resisting and putting your energy into preparing and eating a balanced meal.

Having a balanced diet will make you feel healthier, stronger, mentally sharper, and more confident, all of which are important for helping you overcome your panic attacks. Also, the more you can avoid foods high in sugars and fats, the less of a roller coaster of energy your body will go through. Adopt an ACT mindset: *You* run the show of your life, not your panic attacks, so don't let them get you off course from living a life that promotes good health and nutrition. Consistent with CBT principles, being mindful of what you eat and changing your diet to a healthier, balanced one are active behavioral steps you can take to lessen negative physiological sensations and feelings.

Limit Caffeine, Alcohol, and Nicotine

Caffeine is a stimulant, meaning it is going to increase your heart rate, which is one of the classic symptoms you are trying to reduce in panic disorder. Nicotine is also a stimulant and should be avoided for the same reasons. For tobacco users, nicotine can have a calming effect. The negative health effects of smoking far outweigh the psychological "benefits" of the temporary calm it might bring, so I strongly encourage you to work on reducing or eliminating it entirely. However, given the difficulty of quitting tobacco, it is reasonable if you want to work on your panic attacks first, versus trying to do both at the same time.

Regarding alcohol, many people are able to calm their anxiety and panic by having a drink or two. Although it's okay to drink in moderation, it is more important to identify the function of your drinking behavior to see how it is impacting your panic attacks. One or two drinks at a party to help ease you into a difficult social gathering is not going to hurt you if you aren't an alcoholic and may actually help you connect with others. However, repeated or excessive drinking that is being used to control and avoid panic attacks is only going to prolong your panic disorder, as it is an avoidance behavior, which you'll learn more about in a later chapter.

SLEEP BETTER

Sleep is the foundation for everything else to go better in your life, including your panic attacks with regard to their severity and frequency. Remember, the more rested you feel, the less stressed you will be in general, so when panic hits, you'll be in a better position to deal with it. Review the sleep do's and don'ts to get familiar with some of the steps you can take to get better sleep. Try incorporating a few of the do's and eliminating a few of the don'ts for the next few nights and see how you sleep. You can add some strategies and eliminate other things to see what helps. I understand that panic attacks can be incredibly disruptive to sleep patterns and get some people stuck in cycles of dreading sleep. You can follow these suggestions to try to improve your sleep, but let go of any thoughts about succeeding or failing.

Sleep Do's:

- Move your body or get some exercise during the day.

- Create a bedtime routine, starting about 30 minutes before you go to sleep (preferably not involving screen time).

- Remove distractions, such as your cell phone, laptop, and TV, from your bedroom.

- Keep your bedroom cool, dark, and comfortable as much as possible.

- Go to bed at the same time every night and set your alarm for the same time every morning.

- Listen to calming music or sounds to help you fall asleep.

Sleep Don'ts:

- Don't exercise within one to two hours of bedtime. Exercise stimulates your brain and body, making it more difficult to wind down and fall asleep.

- Don't eat too close to bedtime, especially spicy food. If your digestive system is stimulated, you'll have more difficulty sleeping.

- Don't drink caffeine or other stimulating beverages late in the afternoon.

- Don't take naps because they will throw off your natural sleep cycle. If you are not getting enough sleep at night, a short nap—20 minutes or less—might be okay, but try to avoid napping whenever possible.

- Don't look at or use screens of any kind in bed, such as TV, your phone, or your laptop. The light from these devices can wake up your mind just when you are trying to wind down and fall asleep.

MOVE YOUR BODY

Chances are when you feel anxious, overwhelmed, or stressed, the last thing you want to do is move; you'd probably rather curl up on the couch and decompress. That impulse is understandable, but if you're not moving your body regularly, you're missing out on the benefits of exercise, including building strength, improving cardiovascular health, and releasing positive endorphins in your brain, which can make dealing with panic more tolerable.

If you don't have an exercise routine or something you do regularly that gets your body moving for at least 20 minutes a day, you'll want to start small. Choose a time of day that works for you (in the morning, afternoon, or early evening), and pick something physical that you can do in or near your home. Here are just a few examples:

- Walk (or jog) around the block.

- Watch and follow along with an exercise video suited for your level of fitness.

- Go for a bike ride in your neighborhood.

- Take a yoga class or do some basic yoga poses on your own.

If you commit to making physical activity part of your routine and follow through with it without making excuses or putting it off, it will eventually become a habit. Just start doing it and you will soon see the benefits.

EAT HEALTHIER

What we eat can have a major impact on how we feel. Eating things that make you feel physically bad, drained, "off," or jittery can make panic attacks more likely to occur or harder to cope with when they do happen because now you have more than one challenge to face at once. I'm sure you already know that eating healthier has many benefits, so consider making it a priority. Begin this week by fixing yourself two healthy meals as a first step in making good nutrition a habit. Here's how:

1. Search online for healthy recipes, pick up a food magazine at the grocery store, or borrow a cookbook from a friend or the library.

2. Look at your options and find two simple, affordable, healthy recipes you are interested in trying.

3. Create a list of the ingredients you'll need, and get the items.

4. Set aside time to prepare the meals, preferably when you won't feel too tired to make the effort, such as after a long day at work.

5. Enjoy your meal and refrigerate leftovers for lunch or dinner the next day.

Once you have successfully made yourself one or two meals, try increasing to three meals, and keep improving from there. Also keep healthy snacks around (such as nuts, fruit, veggies, or trail mix), so you aren't tempted by junk food.

THE GREAT OUTDOORS

Getting outside more often can help you retake control of your life by giving you a chance to connect with things in nature that are pleasurable, thereby putting less emphasis on your panic disorder and your fear of having a panic attack. The benefits of the great outdoors include exposure to sunlight (which is necessary for vitamin D production), fresh air, and the opportunity to be mindful of your environment. It can even be fun and evoke positive feelings. Up until the last hundred years, humans spent a lot more time outside. We evolved for outdoor living, hunting and gathering, and eventually, tending our fields and livestock. To get back in touch with this side of yourself, find something fun or interesting to do outside. Here are a couple of ideas you might want to try:

- Walk around a park or the block.

- Sit on a bench or stoop.

- Read outdoors.

- Explore a natural area.

- Ride your bike.

- Participate in a sport.

Go Deeper: Goal Setting for Getting Outside

With the previous strategy in mind, try this in-depth exercise, which helps you develop a plan to get outside by setting a goal and taking the steps to get there. Here are the key components to setting a goal:

1. Identify a problem.

2. State why this problem matters to you.

3. Brainstorm ideas for how to address it.

4. Choose the best solution for you and your schedule.

5. Break it down into concrete, tangible, measurable objectives or steps.

6. Set a time and place for the first step and a general timeline for frequency and duration of ongoing steps.

7. Take the first step and go. Observe any anxiety, panic, or other discomforts that show up. Don't let them stop you, but observe and notice how you feel. **＞**

Let's say that your problem in this regard is that you feel too lazy, anxious, or unmotivated to make it a point to get outside more often. Sometimes staying indoors is both a cause and a symptom of depression, anxiety, and feelings of panic. It becomes cyclical, where panicky feelings lead to avoidance behavior, which leads to more panicky feelings. But you want more for yourself and you know that you can live better and feel better than you do today.

When you brainstorm ideas for how to address this issue, you come up with things like going for a walk or jog around the block, playing an outdoor sport, walking to a nearby store, riding your bike, gardening, sitting on a park bench, and a few other outdoor activities. Any activity you choose can be done solo or with someone else. Now that you've brainstormed a number of possible things you can do outdoors, let's say you decide that the best solution is to go for a walk around your neighborhood.

The steps involved might include getting a pair of comfortable walking shoes, creating a playlist to listen to during your walk, looking ahead at your schedule to see when you're free, checking the weather forecast, and deciding how long you want your walk to be and how far you want to go before turning back. Committing to a time in this case might mean Friday after work at 5:00 p.m. or Saturday morning at 9:00 a.m. Choose a time within seven days so you don't put it off too long or have other things that come up. The general frequency and timeline to start with could be once a week.

When Friday evening or Saturday morning comes around, put on your walking shoes, dress for the weather, and head outside. Don't think about it—just do it.

Everyday Body Awareness

Building body awareness is an important strategy in overcoming panic attacks. Remember, panic attacks are mostly made up of short-lived physiological sensations that, although extremely unpleasant, are not life-threatening. Purposefully engaging your sensory experiences is a starting point for increasing awareness and seeing these panic attacks for what they really are and what they are not.

Mindfulness is an ancient practice that involves nonjudgmental, open observance of your direct experience, both internal and external. With regard to body awareness, start mindfully engaging your brain and noticing your sensory experience. Part of the difficulty with panic attacks is that you can get swept away by catastrophic thoughts, judgments, and assumptions about things that are untrue or unknown. For example, you might feel like the panic attack is never going to end (judgment plus assumption about the future), when really all you know is your direct experience of unpleasant physical sensations in this moment.

So the goal is to take a step back. Take a few deep breaths to slow down your thinking and bring your awareness to the here and now. What are you feeling in *this* moment? If you are in the midst of a panic attack, you might be feeling tingling, numbness, tightness, or heavy pulsing of your heart. Notice the distinction between "My arm is asleep" and "My arm is losing feeling and I think I'm having a heart attack." The key here is nonjudgmental, simple observance of the sensation without turning it into something bigger.

The process of bringing awareness to your senses and physical sensations is going to have a few benefits. Awareness gives you a sense of control over the panic attack. Instead of *I'm losing my mind*, it becomes *I can focus on these sensations and name them*, which then leads to the thought, *I am not losing my mind and I do have some control over where I put my attention and energy right now*. Also, awareness will ground you in the moment and in your direct present experience, instead of letting you get caught up in things that might happen or that could get worse. Practicing awareness will have a calming effect, as well.

Finally, and probably most important, you are actually practicing both acceptance and exposure by being mindful, which are the two biggest skills involved in overcoming panic and anxiety. Instead of letting your behavior be guided by the need to avoid the physical sensations that come with a panic attack and remove yourself (that is, escape) from the situation, your behavior is instead teaching you that you *can* face these unpleasant and uncomfortable sensations, you will still be yourself, and ultimately, you will be okay.

As with learning a new skill, it is better to practice the skill in normal, everyday situations first if you want to be able to rely on them in more difficult, intense situations. You wouldn't be expected to take a math test without practicing the homework problems first. Similarly, there are everyday situations where you can practice mindful awareness to train your brain, so that when panic strikes, you can use one of the following strategies more readily.

MINDFUL MOVEMENT

Become familiar with how your body feels in various states of movement by being mindfully present to the sensations in your body. Learning to pay mindful attention to your body can help you do the same in the midst of a panic attack.

1. Sit comfortably, take a breath or two, and then tune in to your body. What sensations do you notice in your different muscle groups? Is there any tension, heat, or strain, or are your muscles relaxed? Do you notice any sensations in your head? This step will be your point of reference.

2. Now stand up. What sensations do you notice? Where does the blood rush to? What's different now than when you were sitting? How do your feet and legs feel? How does your head feel?

3. Begin walking around your home, mindfully noticing your physical sensations, including your heart rate and breathing, as well as any sensations in your head. As you walk around, you can also open and close cabinets, pick up items, reach up to a shelf, or do similar everyday movements, and note those experiences, as well. Walk mindfully for a few minutes until you have the opportunity to take note of how it feels to move.

PROGRESSIVE MUSCLE RELAXATION

Progressive muscle relaxation is a classic CBT exercise that can have both mindfulness and relaxation benefits. Although the goal is not to relax and get rid of all anxiety, most people still find the experience soothing. Try to stay engaged and present with the sensations you notice in your body. Now is not the time to solve any of life's problems or think about your to-do list. Just focus your awareness on your body.

Find a comfortable place to sit with minimal distractions. You will be progressively tensing and relaxing your muscles from your feet to your head, tensing for five to seven seconds and relaxing for seven to ten seconds. Be careful of any injury-prone areas, skipping them if needed, and do not strain any muscles.

1. Starting with your feet, curl your toes and hold the tension in your feet for five to seven seconds, and then release and relax.

2. Move up to your calves and repeat the flex/hold and release/relax. Continue up your body by engaging the following areas: thighs, buttocks, core/abs, chest, shoulders, arms, hands, neck, face, and head.

3. When you are finished with all of the muscle groups, take a few deep, calming breaths, and just notice the sensations in your body (possibly a warm, relaxed feeling).

Once you have practiced this exercise over time, you can tense and relax for shorter times and practice wherever you are able to sit down.

TAKE A MINDFUL SHOWER

Showers are good times to practice mindfulness because they are loaded with sensory input, which you can simply notice without assigning any meaning. Remember, the idea is to develop nonjudgmental awareness so that when you are in the midst of a panic attack, catastrophic thinking won't be your automatic go-to. You are training yourself to be present with your body and notice, describe, and label the sensations without judgment.

Turn on the shower and notice the steam rising. Step into the shower and feel the water splashing your body. Notice the smells of your soap and shampoo, the sensation of the warm water on your skin, the texture of lotions, the sounds of the water hitting the floor, and the tastes of anything you get in your mouth. These elements are all salient sensory experiences for your mind to focus on. Move intentionally from one sensory input to the next, and observe how you feel throughout your shower.

MINDFUL MEDITATION

Meditation helps you notice your thoughts without getting so attached and consumed by them. It also promotes focus and concentration and has been shown to provide a reduction in anxiety. Practice this meditation daily if you can. Then you can try it when panic shows up. It's a good way to center yourself and change your relationship to distressing thoughts.

1. Sit comfortably in a quiet room and set a timer for three minutes.

2. Close your eyes and take a few deep breaths, in through your nose for a count of four and out through your mouth for a count of four.

3. Now, imagine you are looking up at the sky on a partly cloudy day with a gentle breeze.

4. When a thought pops into your mind, instead of trying to problem solve or react, simply imagine placing the thought on a cloud as it floats by your visual field. Some clouds (and thoughts) might float by quickly, whereas others might pass slowly. Don't try to change them. Simply notice them, put them on the clouds, and observe them passing away.

5. When the timer goes off, open your eyes and take a few more deep breaths.

Meditation can be difficult at first, so be patient with yourself if you had a hard time letting the thoughts go by. We all get hooked by our thoughts from time to time. Your job is to come back to the process of noticing the thoughts with nonjudgmental awareness. You can increase the length of your session and work up to 15 minutes, if you'd like.

TAKEAWAYS

- Panic attacks are sequences of physiological responses that take over the body and involve a rush of different sensations, from sweating and tingling to increased heart rate and dizziness.

- During a panic attack, your body is preparing to fight or escape because it thinks there is a real threat present. It is uncomfortable and unpleasant, but ultimately, this response cannot hurt you.

- Sleep, exercise, and nutrition are great ways to give your body what it needs so that it both maintains a lower baseline level of anxiety and has the most resources ready to manage a panic attack when it comes.

- By getting to know your body and connecting with the experience, you are practicing mindfulness, acceptance, and approach behaviors that will decrease your anxiety and panic over time.

Chapter 3

Your Brain and Panicky Thoughts

The scariness of a panic attack lies not only in the physiological symptoms but also in the catastrophic thoughts that typically accompany them. Our minds like to try to make sense of the world, and if it feels like we're out of control or dying, our thoughts can get pretty dire, as well. The good news is that there are many ways to correct some of the thinking patterns that may cause you to feel terrified during a panic attack. These techniques will provide a sense of grounding and control that can have a calming effect. As with other strategies discussed in this book, the strategies in this chapter will be most effective if you can practice them before, during, and after a panic attack. Some of the cognitive strategies include reframing your thoughts (the process of putting a more reasonable and palatable spin on something that feels pretty aversive at first) and noticing and catching distortions. This chapter is about seeing the tricks your mind is playing on you so that you don't get caught in the trap of believing things to be much worse than they actually are.

What Your Thoughts Tell You about Panic

Your thoughts can tell you all sorts of inaccurate things about what panic attacks are (such as an indication that you are dying) and what you should do in response (escape, avoid, run!). A key strategy here is to analyze both the process and content of your thoughts and thinking patterns so that you can learn to manage distressing thoughts more effectively. By doing so, you can find relief from panic attacks by identifying them for what they actually are, directly changing the content of your thoughts, reframing your thoughts into something more realistic, or just noticing that not all your thoughts are helpful or need to be trusted in any given moment. You'll come to find that the majority of thoughts experienced during a panic attack don't make much sense.

One frustration I hear from so many clients is that they actually know that their thoughts are irrational, but during a panic attack they *feel* so real. How is it that sometimes we can identify thoughts as nonsense, but at other times the same thought can have us rushing to the emergency room, convinced we are having a heart attack? The difficulty we face is the interaction of the thoughts with the physiological reactions of a panic attack, which ultimately feed the thoughts and make them worse.

Your brain wants to keep you safe. To do so, it looks out for the biggest threats or dangers. For instance, having a heart attack would require urgent attention, so your brain thinks through this possibility immediately to try to spur you to action. For others, maybe they have figured out they are not having a heart attack, but they have more of a fear of "losing their mind" or losing control. Again, the panic attack feels very unmanageable, so it makes sense to have thoughts of being powerless. Add that feeling to the mind's great ability to predict and plan for the future, and you start telling yourself, *This is it. I'm never going to be in control again. What is going to happen to me?*

A great advantage of being human is that our minds have evolved to be efficient problem-solving machines. The downside of being human during a panic attack is that the mind applies this same logic and looks for the cause and then a solution. Is it a closed-in space, performance situation, noise, highway, or crowded event that is the source of this panic? And if so, can we avoid panic by escaping and avoiding these situations entirely? Seems like a pretty airtight story, and all we have to do is follow our mind's advice to keep ourselves safe, right? But again, the problem here is that we are treating the panic attacks as actual dangers and threats, when in reality they are not.

Your thoughts might start telling you to avoid airplanes and you'll be fine, or perhaps your mind says that if you just lay low during a meeting or in class, you can escape the ordeal without being put on the spot. Another common fear your mind might drum up is that if you join a conversation, people will think you are weird or boring, so you're better off staying quiet or maybe just skipping gatherings altogether. Sure, these thoughts seem pretty reasonable: Avoid a difficult situation whenever possible and prevent the panic attacks. Maybe your thoughts take it to the next level of telling you to try to avoid *all* situations that make you nervous. These thoughts can feel so real because you've already had the experience of a panic attack in one or more of these situations, so of course you want to look for a logical solution to minimize panic in the future.

The problem, of course, is that giving in to these thoughts reinforces them and makes them stronger and more believable. So, you need to look for ways to get out of the thought trap so that these thoughts, which are actually largely untrue, do not take over your life. The following strategies build upon one another to help you along.

REFLECT ON YOUR THOUGHTS

To gain a better understanding of what your mind does during a panic attack, take a moment to reflect on your last episode specifically with regard to what you were thinking at the time. Try to approach this exercise without judgment. The idea is not to relive the event in your mind but to observe in your memory what occurred. Recalling your last panic attack, answer the following questions:

- What thoughts and/or fears came to mind?

- Did you experience any thoughts related to your physical safety and well-being?

- Did you experience any thoughts related to your mental well-being or sense of control?

RATE YOUR FEARS

To confidently take on your fears, a good strategy is to look at them honestly and openly. Rating your fears will help you identify which fearful thoughts are causing you the most distress and are most likely to hold you back in different situations.

1. In the previous strategy, you identified the thoughts or fears that came to mind during your last panic attack. Rate each fearful thought from 1 to 10, with 1 being the least frightening and 10 being the most frightening. When rating the fears, think about how scary they felt to you in the moment.

2. Identify which thoughts you've given the highest score. Do these thoughts feel scary right now when you are thinking about them or only during a panic attack?

Now that you have rated and reflected on your fears, you have a better idea of which cause you the most concern. You can start tackling the most troublesome thoughts first.

IDENTIFY UNHELPFUL COMMANDS

Do you know what advice your mind is giving you either in response to panic or in anticipation of another panic attack? Is it telling you to avoid certain places, public events, situations, meetings, social events, shopping malls, concerts, bridges, highways, closed-in spaces, or somewhere else? Is your mind telling you to start researching everything you can about heart attacks or schizophrenia to see if you have any of the signs that you are in danger of a serious physical or mental health condition? Or perhaps it is telling you that you can't travel anymore or leave the house for any reason that isn't absolutely necessary.

Reflect on five situations where your mind might be telling you to avoid certain things because you are anticipating a panic attack, as well as any other commands it is giving you with regard to panic.

PRACTICE SELF-COMPASSION

Panic attacks may make you feel weak, broken, and inferior, when in fact, none of this is true. Remember, you are strong for picking up this book and taking on these challenges to deal with your panic attacks. So, take a few minutes now to intentionally channel some compassion to yourself by considering these questions:

- What are some kind things you can tell yourself about your own self-worth?

- Which aspects of yourself do you feel most positive about?

- What do you believe you are capable of?

Are you noticing that you almost have two minds—one that is negative and telling you that you can't do anything, but another one that knows there is more to the story and that you are capable of so much more, the one you just connected with? Remember that not everything your mind tells you is true, and that by being more compassionate with yourself, the negative part of you will have less sway over your feelings about yourself.

Common Thinking Errors

There are many common thinking patterns that we may experience related to panic attacks. The CBT community has organized some of these thought patterns into categories to make them easier to identify and address, such as filtering out positive information, jumping to conclusions, and getting caught up in worst-case scenarios. The better you become at recognizing your own thought patterns, the better you are going to be at tackling them, letting them go, seeing the reality of the situation, and responding more effectively. As you read these descriptions, consider whether you may have fallen into one or more of these traps.

A common theme throughout these thinking errors, or distortions, is an overemphasis on the negatives in a situation. As explained earlier, your brain is designed to keep you safe, so it is going to look for negative or dangerous situations and threats while oftentimes ignoring the positives and safety cues that are more realistic in most situations. By understanding this pattern, you can avoid getting stuck in the negatives. According to psychologist John M. Grohol, there are 15 common cognitive distortions. I'll discuss the five that are most relevant to panic, and then you'll have an opportunity to practice some strategies to work through these common thinking errors.

Filtering

With filtering, essentially your mind decides that it will save you some mental energy by ignoring what it deems unimportant (that is, those things that are safe, benign, or positive) and instead focusing on the perceived negatives and dangers. An example is the thought, *I am trapped on this airplane, and I have no escape*, which conveniently filters out thoughts (or facts of the situation) such as *I am sitting here just like everyone else, flying is statistically one of the safest activities, the flight attendants seem calm, and no one else is reacting to any crisis.* Your goal is to intentionally broaden your thinking to see if there are neutral or positive factors in the situation that may be getting filtered out prematurely.

Polarized Thinking

The second distortion is known as "black-and-white" thinking, or polarized thinking. In this case, the mind decides that a situation is either all good or all bad. There is nothing in between. For example, in a social situation, have you ever thought that because someone didn't laugh or smile at your joke, it means they hate you? This type of automatic thought pattern could quickly spiral into a panic attack at work or a social gathering. In this example, the mind is declaring that either someone loves you and will demonstrate their love at all times or they hate you. And because they are doing something neutral, the absence of the positive leads your mind to the negative conclusion that they hate you. The reality, of course, is that life and especially interpersonal interactions are full of gray areas that are not dangerous or negative, and we don't need to fear them or always assume the worst.

Control Fallacies

Control fallacies are beliefs that you should be able to control things that you have no power over, including the physiological symptoms of a panic attack. With panic disorder, there's also often a preoccupation with needing to control and predict the outcome of a situation, including how everyone else is feeling, what they are thinking, and what they will do, even though these things are inherently unknowable. Control fallacies lead to frustration and fear because many things are not actually in your power, which then reinforces the panic.

Overgeneralizing

With overgeneralizing, your mind becomes focused on one incident (typically something negative) and assumes that this is how it always is and always will be in the future. For example, if you panic while on a date, and your date seems judgmental, your mind generalizes that anyone you date will be judgmental, so what's the point in dating? As much as it feels like it, you cannot predict the future, so don't let your mind even try. One incident does not make a trend, and one person is not a representative sample of all people. Also, one panic attack during a date does not mean you will always have a panic attack in that situation.

Catastrophizing

Probably the biggest cognitive distortion when it comes to panic attacks is catastrophizing. Catastrophizing is when your mind jumps ahead to that worst-case scenario and believes it to be the case here and now, when it actually is not true and is unlikely to come true. The classic case is believing you are having a heart attack (catastrophe) when in actuality your heart is beating faster and you are noticing some tingling in one arm. There are other explanations, such as your body having an anxiety/fear response, that don't have anything to do with having a heart attack and dying, yet your mind seems unable to see the less extreme interpretation. So, next time, try slowing down and noticing that maybe things aren't actually as bad as your mind would have you believe.

WHAT'S MY COGNITIVE DISTORTION?

Think of five common thoughts you tend to get stuck on related to panic attacks and anxiety, whether during an attack or just generally. Look back at the descriptions of the cognitive distortions. Do any of the thoughts you just identified fall into those categories? If you feel stuck in your struggle against panic and hopeless about your ability to make improvements, consider how this feeling may be another distortion. Consider if you are actually filtering out positive experiences in your life or overgeneralizing one or more difficult situations to declare that they happen "everywhere" or "all the time."

Take a moment now to remind yourself that you are not your thoughts. You may have been trapped by a distortion because that is the pathway that your mind has carved out and practiced for years. The good news is that the brain is malleable, and there many other ways of looking at different situations. Noticing and increasing awareness of how your thoughts work is a first step toward responding to them differently so that they have less power over you and elicit less anxiety the next time.

TEST THE HYPOTHESIS

Some common thinking errors related to panic involve the length of time the panic attack is going to last, your ability to handle it, and your assumption of how everyone else is going to respond if you start panicking. A good intervention against these distortions is called hypothesis testing. Test yourself to see just how long your panic symptoms last at maximum intensity, whether or not you made it out alive (you did!), and how others responded to the situation. After your next panic attack, try to answer the following questions:

- How long did the symptoms last? Was it an hour? Did they last forever?

- Did you experience a thought like *I just can't take it if this gets any worse*? What does "I just can't take it" actually mean? Were you going to spontaneously combust? Put this thought to the test. What could you literally not take? Did you really lose control?

- Did everyone else notice and care that you were anxious? Remember, anxiety feels a thousand times worse to you on the inside, but people on the outside rarely notice and might not even care if they do notice. Sure, you may have elevated breathing or sweating, or look noticeably uncomfortable, but again, there's no need to put so much value on these things. Remember the ACT principle of taking steps toward things you actually care about (your values), even if they come with some negative feelings or discomfort, including temporary embarrassment.

QUESTION THE REALITY OF THE PROBLEM

Think of a time when you started panicking in front of other people. Do you recall anyone noticing that you were having a panic attack? The majority of the time, people are more focused on themselves. So, is panicking in public actually a problem? I would argue, no, it is not. I admit that I don't like feeling embarrassed or panicky any more than the next person, but my life would be a lot narrower if I avoided every situation where I might experience these things.

Also, were your physiological symptoms actually a problem once the attack passed? Many of them are similar to what one experiences while exercising, but we don't call them a problem in that context. Panic sucks, and I know you've picked up this book to try to stop panicking, so I want to drive this point home: You can take steps to ground yourself in reality and build confidence in your ability to handle the symptoms of panic. Here's the strategy:

1. **Normalize:** Remind yourself that these physical symptoms are not harmful bodily functions and responses.

2. **Accept:** Accept the temporary discomfort that comes with these symptoms because you cannot change them in the moment.

3. **Approach:** Approach situations that may expose you to the symptoms to take away their power over you.

These steps train your mind to see your panic attacks more realistically—as not that big of a problem. Reframe your cognitive distortions, which I'll discuss soon, to help motivate you to accept and approach your symptoms.

DON'T ENGAGE WITH THAT THOUGHT

Another great cognitive strategy is to train your mind not to engage with the thoughts in the first place. Our minds can be pretty good lawyers at times, and even when you fight the distortions and present the evidence that things are going to be okay, your mind still may find a way to say, "But what about *that* feeling?" or "What if this gets worse and I can't handle it?" These thoughts can be hard to battle because we don't know what the future will bring, and yet our minds desperately want certainty and answers now. Try the strategy below:

1. Notice the thought. Take a step back and decide to not engage with it.

2. Practice saying to yourself, "I'm noticing I'm having the thought that [*insert thought*]." For example, instead of saying to yourself, "I'm having a panic attack and it's going to ruin this event," you could say, "I'm noticing I'm having the thought that this panic attack is going to ruin everything." Notice here that I'm not asking you to change or judge the thought. Instead, I am encouraging you to just watch your mind as it wants to race ahead, jump to conclusions, and engage in the rest of the distortions.

3. Stay present and be an observer. Just notice the thoughts without being consumed by them (remember your mindfulness strategies from chapter 2).

Go Deeper: Keep a Thought Log

Familiarize yourself with the table on the next page. You can re-create this table in a blank document on your computer and print it out or draw one by hand in your notebook or journal. This table will be your thought log. The next time you have a panic attack or worry that you are going to have a panic attack, record the thoughts you were having in the first column. See if you can figure out what the distortion was. Question whether the thought was true and if it was actually a problem. What might be a more realistic interpretation of the situation?

Here's an example: You are having a panic attack on an airplane and you think, *I feel trapped and I'm going to suffocate.* The distortion is an example of catastrophizing—your mind is taking the sensation of feeling trapped and turning it into a bigger issue: *I'm going to suffocate.* In this case, it is true that you feel trapped; you are on an airplane and you cannot leave. The part that is untrue is that you are going to suffocate, because fresh air is being circulated throughout the plane. Is this scenario actually a problem? Everyone else is "trapped," too, and they seem to be breathing just fine. If you commit to the experience of feeling trapped, do you think it may actually start to decrease at any point in the next 10 to 20 minutes? What if you start doing an activity, such as working on a puzzle, watching a movie, or listening to music? Now, is the feeling of being suffocated still present? Mark down how else you might interpret this situation and the reality of what is happening to you.

Here's another example: You need to go the grocery store. The thought that you "always" have panic attacks in grocery stores pops up. This distortion is an example of overgeneralizing, perhaps based on a previous experience. So, is it true? Even if you have had a panic attack in a grocery store, you can't be sure it will *always* happen. So you'd answer no. Is having a panic attack in the store actually a problem? The reality of the situation is that if you don't go to the store, you won't get what you need. With this more realistic interpretation of the situation, the idea of acceptance and approach comes in again: "I feel like I could panic and lose my mind if I go back to that store, and I don't want to feel that, but I bet I could actually get through it and still get what I need." Now it's your turn. Keep a thought log for the next few weeks and observe how it is helping you maintain control over your panic.

THOUGHT	DISTORTION	IS IT ACTUALLY TRUE?	IS IT ACTUALLY A PROBLEM?	MORE REALISTIC INTERPRETATION
Things are starting to feel "unreal," which means I'm developing schizophrenia.	Catastrophizing, filtering (I actually am still in reality, but my focus is all on this one scary feeling)	No	No—a feeling is not a problem.	This feeling is scary, unpleasant, and uncomfortable, but not actually a sign that I am psychotic. I am still me and can stay present with this feeling.

Learning to Reframe

By now you have some idea that maybe not everything your mind tells you is true or helpful. We all get stuck in negative thought patterns, and if you're suffering from panic attacks, they can be even more difficult. Fortunately, there are other strategies that can be even more effective for navigating negative and scary thoughts. One strategy is called cognitive restructuring, or reframing. This technique is essentially taking pieces of what your mind is giving you and thinking about them in a different, less scary, more tolerable way. With some cognitive distortions, your mind is giving you completely false information, so you want to treat it as such by being more dismissive of the information. However, with other scary thoughts that may have some truth to them, you want to acknowledge that truth but also see the bigger picture. There is usually a nicer, more palatable way of describing something that may help ease your nerves.

Here's a classic example: Instead of asking in a job interview what an applicant's weaknesses are, the interviewer asks, "What are your areas for growth?" Does everyone have things they are not good at? Of course! Do we need to call them "weaknesses" and take on all the associated baggage of that term? No. So, instead we say "areas for growth" because that is technically what they are. They are areas where someone could improve to be a better employee.

One key reframing skill is making sure you are labeling a behavior and not a character trait. There is a big difference between the statements "I am an anxious person" and "I struggle with panic attacks." In the first statement, your story has been defined, you are an anxious person, and there is nothing you will be able to do to change that. In this second one, you are correctly labeling that you are not equal to panic attacks, you are not defined by your panic attacks, and they are something you struggle with (right now). You may have struggled with many things throughout your life, especially when starting out. Many people struggle with subjects in school, exercise, making friends, a sport, cooking, or a foreign language. However, if they stick with it and practice, they get better. The story can change.

How many of us struggle with the following notion? *Anxiety is pointless and annoying, and I wish I could get rid of it.* If you broaden your horizon about where anxiety comes from, you might come to this cognitive reframe: *Anxiety shows up whenever I am challenged, in a new environment, or engaged in something I care about (and therefore not wanting it to go poorly).* Wouldn't you rather have a life that involves challenge, growth, new opportunities, and meaningful engagement? If so, then you can welcome anxiety, not avoid it.

Cognitive restructuring shows us that we are not concrete beings and that anxiety and panic are not concrete entities living inside us. Instead, we are constantly growing, adapting, and learning how to navigate the world, people, emotions, and everything else. Here are a few more examples of relevant cognitive reframes:

- *The physical symptoms of panic attacks are very similar to engaging in heavy exercise, not just having a heart attack.*

- *Anxiety, nervous energy, and excitement are all very similar emotional and physical experiences, yet for some reason we try so hard to get rid of the first two whereas we celebrate the last one.*

CATCH THE NEGATIVE THOUGHT AND REFRAME IT

Now it's your turn to try. Think of at least three negative thoughts you have been struggling with—either before, during, or after a panic attack. Let's see if you can reframe them. Here are a couple examples to get you started:

- Thought: *My life is over if these panic attacks continue.*
  Reframe: *Panic attacks are a challenge that I have to face right now, and life will go on.*

- Thought: *I am so weak.*
  Reframe: *I have many strengths, and when I learn and practice strategies to deal with panic attacks, I will be even stronger.*

Come up with a reframe for each thought you've been struggling with. Each day this week, reframe three different thoughts to start shifting your pattern of thinking.

GIVE YOUR NEGATIVE THOUGHT A FUNNY VOICE

That nagging, negative voice in your head probably sounds pretty harsh and serious, doesn't it? When you notice that you are having a negative thought, state your thought aloud. But instead of saying it in your regular voice, say it in a funny tone or with a thick accent. You can imitate the voice of a cartoon character or famous actor, such as Arnold Schwarzenegger in *The Terminator*. You can raise the pitch of your voice while speaking really fast or speak very slowly, like Lurch in *The Addams Family*. Play around with it and have some fun.

This technique is an ACT strategy for dealing with negative thoughts. The idea here is to take your negative thoughts less seriously and see them for the jumble of words that they are, not absolute truths about you, the world, or the future. The words remain the same, but the impact they have can be changed based on your perception of them.

LOOK FOR EVERYDAY EXAMPLES OF REFRAMES

To reinforce your ability to reframe your negative thoughts surrounding a panic attack, begin to look out for examples of reframing in everyday life. One excellent example is TV commercials. Advertisers know that when they frame their wares in a positive light, consumers are more likely to buy their product. Think of a car commercial where the car is touted as being a safe, luxurious ride. They aren't focusing on the high monthly payments or the cost of insuring a luxury car. Consider, too, the family that's sharing a bag of chips in the park: The commercial doesn't mention their high calorie content. The next time you are watching a commercial, see if you can pick out reframes like this.

Politicians are also experts at reframing: They can generally look at the same set of facts as their opponents and reframe them into an argument that supports their position. Reframing is a useful tool in many contexts, so the better you get at identifying it and doing it, the more effective it will be when you're in the middle of a panic attack and need to reframe your thoughts.

NOTICE WHEN OTHERS NEED A REFRAME

When you're first learning to reframe, it might be easier to recognize when other people are making negative statements that could use a good reframe. Consider the friend who says, "I really suck at the piano. I've been taking lessons, but I'm getting nowhere." Keep in mind that your friend just might want to vent, and of course you can say something supportive, but mentally note how they could turn that comment into a positive statement: "I'm motivated to take piano lessons so that I can get better at it." Or let's say your coworker tells you they're afraid of seeming like a failure because they're still single after a recent breakup. You could reframe their singledom by pointing out that you see them as independent, brave, or interesting. Remember, sometimes people just want to vent or need some validation, so simply practice thinking to yourself how to restructure their comments. With someone very close to you, you can practice reframing aloud if they're open to it.

Go Deeper: Make a Game Plan for Working with Your Thoughts

So far, you've learned about cognitive distortions and cognitive restructuring. For these strategies to make a difference during a panic attack, you need to put them into practice ahead of time and in everyday life, especially when you are not panicking. Then, when you are going into a situation where you fear you might panic, you will already be able to pull out one of these tools to help take the edge off of your panic and anxiety. None of these strategies are going to eliminate panic attacks or the anxiety you might feel heading into a difficult situation. However, they are designed to give you a little more breathing room, increase your confidence, and provide more tools in your toolbox when panic does strike.

Are some negative thoughts still going to be there? Sure. But do they have to stop you and limit your life? Absolutely not. So, take a few minutes now to think about your week ahead. What kinds of situations are already making you nervous? What thoughts are running through your mind about those situations? Are there any distortions in there to catch? Is there another, less extreme way of looking at the scenario ahead that might help you out?

How are you going to start keeping track of your thoughts? Are you going to keep a thought log? If so, are you going to use it every morning, at lunchtime, in the evening, or right before bed? Pick a time that makes sense with your schedule, energy levels, and other commitments, and stick to it. Planning a schedule explicitly makes it more likely for you to follow through. Write out your game plan in your notebook or your device now. Check back daily to make sure you are following through as planned.

TAKEAWAYS

- Our thoughts are often inaccurate, especially when it comes to panic attacks.

- Remember to question your thoughts: How true are they, how much of the picture are you really seeing, and is what they are telling you really a problem that you cannot handle?

- Getting to know your thoughts can help you start picking out the cognitive distortions, those common negative pitfalls that your mind is susceptible to.

- Reframe your thoughts in a positive way, such as seeing panic as more of a challenge to conquer than a problem that ruins everything.

- Practicing your strategies in everyday life can help you use those tools when panic occurs.

Chapter 4

Your Behavior and Fear-Based Avoidance

I firmly believe that changing your behavior is the single best thing you can do to manage your panic attacks. This chapter is all about getting out of the "avoidance trap" and facing your panic attacks head-on so that you can live the life you deserve in spite of them. Although avoidance can sometimes feel like the safer choice in the moment, it keeps you stuck in patterns that ultimately reinforce your anxiety and panic, usually making matters worse over time. In this chapter, I'll talk about these patterns and give you real strategies to break this cycle. ACT is all about reducing avoidance and taking active behavioral steps toward your values while also helping you develop tolerance for distressing emotions and sensations. Although some of the strategies in this chapter may sound scary, I promise you that the more you practice them, the easier it gets. You will learn through your direct experience that you can handle the situations that felt so scary and that you had been previously avoiding.

The Avoidance Trap

When discussing avoidance, I am referring to anything you do to escape and avoid panic and anxiety about thoughts, feelings, sensations, memories, situations, people, places, events, and more. Humans evolved to avoid anything we perceive as dangerous, which is extremely adaptive because it protects us from harm and keeps us vigilant. However, as you have been learning, anxious minds often make up threats or perceive them where there are none. When you're in the grip of panic, you are likely to see those threats as catastrophic and life-threatening. If you let your panicky thoughts guide your decisions about where is safe to go or what is safe to do, your life can become increasingly constricted.

The tricky thing about avoidance behavior is that it seems to work in the short term, which makes it that much more reinforcing and appealing. For example, say you are invited out to dinner and worry that you will have a panic attack at the restaurant; your mind might tell you that you could pass out or throw up in front of dozens of people and be humiliated. In this case, it's possible you would rather just skip going out to eat and stay home to avoid the panic attack. Staying in relieves the anxiety and panic in the moment. This calming effect feels good, so you are more likely to continue doing it over time. However, the downside is it reinforces and strengthens the belief in your mind that (a) you definitely would have had a panic attack at the restaurant, and (b) something humiliating would have happened. Now life has gotten narrower because you feel you can no longer go to restaurants. And, because of the way our minds have evolved to learn about dangers in the world, you may start to fear going to any public place where there are other people you could be humiliated in front of, such as a movie theater, bank, or store.

Avoidance might work in the short term, but it shrinks your life and strengthens anxiety over time. The inaccurate beliefs you were trying to challenge and think about differently in chapter 3 grow stronger when you avoid certain situations. Conversely, the less you avoid, the more you are letting your direct experience teach you that these beliefs are actually false predictions and catastrophic exaggerations, and you do not need to buy into them.

It's important to remember that avoidance behavior is hardwired into us. Back in the days of our early ancestors, the ones who avoided leaving the cave and going to the watering hole until it was as safe as possible are the ones who survived. They may have gone hungry or thirsty for a bit longer, but the keen sense of avoiding danger is what kept them and their families alive for generations. These are the people we evolved from, and thus, we, too, are on the lookout for dangers. Modern society is fortunately safer than the environments our ancestors lived in, but our systems have not caught up to that fact yet. If it feels like our life is in danger (even when we may "know" it is not), our instinct to escape and avoid is still strong. So, there is no shame in the fact that you may be stuck in this avoidance cycle. I want you to be kind to yourself, not judgmental, for struggling here. Remember, it happens to everyone.

There are two levels of avoidance that are problematic. The obvious one is avoiding situations, such as stores or social events, where you might experience a panic attack. The second level, which is more subtle, is the internal avoidance of your thoughts, feelings, and sensations happening inside your body. Although this concept may seem strange at first, it is important to note here that a large part of the problem with panic is the attempt at suppressing, controlling, and escaping the physical sensations of the panic attack. If it were so easy to just turn off the panic, you wouldn't be reading this book in the first place. Mindfulness, acceptance, and exposure to the sensations will offer alternatives to the instinctual attempt to escape uncomfortable feelings in your body and mind.

LOOK AT YOUR AVOIDANCE

The first step to challenging your avoidance behaviors is to identify their features and characteristics. Doing so will lay the groundwork for the other strategies in this chapter. Looking at your avoidance behaviors is a necessary first step in ACT to stop avoiding and start approaching fear and discomfort, which will give you increased flexibility over time. Spend a few minutes mindfully reflecting on your answers to these questions:

- What situations do you find yourself avoiding? In what way(s) do you tend to avoid them?

- Do you avoid anticipatory anxiety (fear and dread of what's to come)? What do you usually do to avoid it?

- What thoughts, feelings, and sensations in your body do you try to escape or avoid?

- What do you get out of avoidance? In other words, what are the benefits you experience (for example, a sense of calm or relief)?

- If you were to stop avoiding, what would you have to give up?

RECALL SOME WINS

Recalling wins promotes flexible thinking and contacting the positive emotions that come from taking chances and accomplishing your goals (which can often be overlooked by negative patterns of thinking). Think about a few times in your life when you chose not to avoid something and the experience contributed to your life in some way, big or small. Here are two examples to get you started:

- *It was my very first day of school, and I was nervous. As much as I wanted to run away from the big, scary school bus, I got on anyway, and then I went on to learn new stuff and make new friends.*

- *I was dreading going to my friend's surprise birthday party, and I thought about making up some excuse why I couldn't be there, but I went anyway. I ended up having an amazing time.*

Spend some time searching your memory for examples like these. When you've thought of them, no matter how insignificant they may seem to you, give yourself credit for overcoming the urge to avoid the situation. Appreciate the good outcomes that came from your decision to go for it despite not wanting to.

RECALL SOME STRUGGLES

Recalling struggles is a move toward accepting that not everything goes our way in life and that there are areas we can improve if we are honest with ourselves and put in the effort. So, now that you have a few wins under your belt, think about a few times in your life when you did avoid the situation or event. How did it feel to avoid the situation? What was the cost to you? Do you think you are better or worse off for having avoided this event? Here is an example to get you started:

> *I declined a free ticket to see my favorite band because I was afraid of having a panic attack in the concert hall. I felt relief that I declined, but I missed out on what I later heard was an incredible concert. Being able to see the band would have deepened my appreciation of their music, so I would have been better off if I had gone.*

The idea is not to make yourself feel bad about avoiding the event or situation but to reflect on the honest toll that avoidance took on your life, which can motivate you to try something different next time. Here are a couple of quick ideas for what to try next time:

- Call or text a friend to get a little confidence boost going into the situation.

- Do a quick mindfulness exercise to calm and ground yourself (such as the body scan on page 22).

- Think of a cognitive reframe (see page 57) to try to see the situation as less scary.

BE KIND TO YOURSELF

Being kind to yourself is consistent with ACT principles of acceptance and mindfulness and the CBT principle of looking at the whole picture instead of getting caught up in negative judgments about yourself. Learning to deal with your panic and anxiety head-on (that is, without your avoidance behaviors) is an incredibly difficult process, especially when it comes to panic attacks. It is easy to get stuck on the negative thoughts of how hard it is, so you need to intentionally remind yourself to be kind to yourself by using positive self-talk. Yes, the avoidance pathways in your brain are strong, but you are stronger. What are some kind things you can say to yourself when you feel like the steps you are taking are too difficult? Here are some ideas:

- *Even though I'm finding this difficult, I am stronger than I realize.*

- *I've accomplished things in my life that I am proud of, and I can accomplish this, too.*

- *I am learning new strategies, even if I'm not doing them perfectly.*

- *They might be hard now, but new behaviors will get easier the more I practice them.*

Come up with a few of your own or use these, and repeat them to yourself when you need to. If you think you'll forget them, jot them down on a sticky note or in your notes app on your phone or other device.

Go Deeper: Acceptance

Acceptance is the single most important thing to master with regard to anxiety disorders and other mental health issues. Acceptance is best conceptualized as an active process—a willingness to feel how you really feel. It's not about sugarcoating things or escaping reality; it's about embracing the truth that comes from stressful events in life. You have likely already been exposed to situations throughout your life that required acceptance, so you've already got some experience in this area.

Recall the first time you lost someone close to you, maybe a grandparent or other relative, friend, or even a beloved pet. The grieving process is all about acceptance and processing emotions. You could try to live in denial or engage in self-destructive behaviors (e.g., excessive substance abuse) to numb the pain, but ultimately, we all come to a place where we need to accept pain in our lives, such as the pain of losing someone. Another example would be to think about a time when you were disappointed by an outcome or experienced rejection—receiving a bad grade on a test, not getting the job you wanted, or being turned down for a date by someone you really liked. Any time something in life doesn't work out the way you wanted or hoped for, it comes with some sort of pain or realization of loss, and in comes acceptance.

This same practice can be applied to anxiety and panic, not just grief, loss, and disappointment. The difference here is that acceptance seems like more of a choice when it comes to confronting panic. As discussed, you could choose to go on avoiding panic and not accepting the discomfort. However, that choice comes with such a high cost that I hope you start to see it as no choice at all. Acceptance and the willingness to feel your panic and anxiety openly, honestly, and nonjudgmentally are the way out. The ACT community uses several metaphors to describe acceptance. One really impactful metaphor I like to use is the idea of being trapped in quicksand. >

When stuck in quicksand, it is our instinct to panic and start flailing about, trying to escape as quickly as possible (sound familiar?). However, the most effective strategy is to stop, accept that you are in a scary situation, and actually lay yourself across it, contacting it fully, rather than trying to immediately escape and avoid it. The less you resist the quicksand (and your panic), the better off you are. Then, you can come up with a plan and take effective action to get through the panic attack. Think back to an unpleasant experience and practice "laying yourself across it." In other words, practice letting go of the struggle to change the situation and just feel your feelings. After you've had some practice, you can try this strategy during a panic attack.

Alternatives to Avoidance and Escape

The main alternatives to avoidance and escape are approach and acceptance. These strategies are the best ways to overcome panic. Only you can give yourself the direct experience you need to see that you are more resilient than you realized and that panic attacks can't actually hurt you. We took a good look at acceptance in the Go Deeper section on page 69, and you'll have an opportunity to practice what acceptance feels like. Now, I want to spend a little time discussing approach behavior, and then another alternative to avoidance and escape: distraction.

Approach behavior can look like a lot of different things, so I'll break it down into smaller steps that may feel more manageable. Begin with the understanding that avoidance isn't black-and-white behavior; rather, it varies across a continuum from avoidance all the way to approach. For instance, when confronting the fear of panic attacks at a shopping mall, you could completely avoid going to malls, thinking about malls, or doing anything in your life related to malls (outright avoidance). On the other end of the spectrum, you might fully confront your fear of panic attacks by going to the shopping mall on the most crowded day while wearing a T-shirt that says, "Please ask me about my panic attacks" (one example of an outright approach). Other behaviors can fall anywhere on the spectrum, leaning more toward avoidance, more toward approach, or somewhere in the middle.

When figuring out alternatives to avoidance, be sure to classify your approach behaviors by their function, not their form. To make this distinction, ask yourself, "What am I really up to?" If you are trying to face your anxiety around having a panic attack in a store, you can check in with yourself: "Am I running errands on a Tuesday evening because that's when the stores are less crowded and I am trying to avoid people? Or am I running errands on a Tuesday evening because that is the only time my schedule allows for me to go? Is running errands a big first step in finding an alternative to my avoidance behavior? Or have I already been going to these particular stores, and thus, is going on a Tuesday evening really helping me avoid my true fear of being around people?" Be aware that this same approach behavior may be serving different functions depending on where you are in the process and how much panic or anxiety something evokes in you.

Another alternative to avoidance is distraction. As I mentioned earlier, many behaviors may lie somewhere between outright avoidance and outright approach. For example, let's say you are at home and start to feel the beginnings of a panic attack coming on. As a distraction, you turn on a funny online video, play a video game, or listen to some music. Are you fully facing all of the panicky thoughts, feelings, and sensations? Not exactly. But are you heading to the emergency room or self-medicating? No. Sometimes distractions are helpful when the anxiety peaks and you just don't feel up to doing a full approach in the moment.

When you're out in public and feeling like a panic attack might strike, there are some distractions you might engage in to mitigate some of the intensity of the anxiety. Perhaps you stand in the corner and check your phone. Another distraction might be excusing yourself from a social situation and going to the restroom, just to give yourself a break. You're not leaving the situation entirely (avoidance), and you're also doing what you can to not fully face the experience you are having.

So, although different alternatives to avoidance are more or less direct approaches to panicky feelings, and consequently more or less scary, I am in favor of anything that helps you stop avoiding. Avoidance is the behavior that comes with the highest cost to your life, narrowing and restricting it while strengthening the anxiety. Approach, acceptance, and even distraction are all tools that can be pulled out to help keep you moving toward your goals and reducing avoidance in your life. Try a few of the following strategies to see what works best for you as alternatives to avoidance and escape.

YOUR DISTRACTION TOOLBOX

If you're struggling with panic attacks and anxiety at home, and it feels like they are just taking over your life, then it's a good idea to get some tools together to help you work through these situations and gain confidence. Some examples might be playing a game on your phone, doing a relaxation exercise, watching a video online, reading an article, walking outside, or playing with a pet. Distractions don't make all the anxiety go away, but they give your brain something else to focus on besides the panic, which is helpful in breaking the panic cycle.

Take a minute now and think about three distractions you can engage in the next time panic strikes and you just need a break. Remember to not become dependent on these attempts at escaping and controlling your panic, but rather, think of them as little mini vacations you are giving your mind. Try different distraction activities to see which ones are most effective for you.

DEEP-BREATHING EXERCISE

Often, one of the symptoms of panic attacks is shallow breathing. With this strategy, you get to take back a little bit of control and regulate your breathing. This technique helps bring the rest of your mind back "online" to then be better able to reframe your negative thoughts (see page 57). Practice this skill frequently, and then pull it out when fears of having a panic attack arise or an actual panic attack comes.

Stop wherever you are and just breathe. Focus on taking long, deep breaths in through your nose for a count of four and then long, slow exhales for a count of six. As you breathe in, imagine filling your diaphragm, or belly, with air like a balloon. And then slowly let it out, deflating the balloon. Do this exercise at least three times or for as long as you feel the need to. Remember, your only job is to breathe; don't worry about anything else.

5-4-3-2-1 GROUNDING EXERCISE

This is a good grounding exercise to turn to when you notice panic building or are in the midst of a panic attack. The idea is to ground yourself in the here and now and stop your mind from running away to some future catastrophe. You can practice silently in your head wherever you are. Here are the steps:

1. Name five things you can see right now.

2. Name four things you can hear right now.

3. Name three things you can touch right now.

4. Name two things you can smell right now.

5. Name one thing you can taste right now.

This exercise gets you back in touch with your direct experience through your senses. After you're finished, you might notice that you feel a little calmer or more in control.

JUST SIT WITH IT

What do you mean, just sit with it? I know, it sounds too simple, but one of the best alternatives to avoidance is acceptance. The next time a panic-related feeling comes up at home or when you are out in the world, instead of jumping into problem-solving mode, just stop, take a deep breath, and see if you can sit and do nothing. Simply sit in a chair and don't focus on doing anything to change the situation. Just be with yourself and your panic attack. As my old professor used to say, "In doing nothing, something gets done." The something that gets done is an important lesson in acceptance of unpleasant and uncomfortable thoughts, feelings, and sensations. It also allows for some hypothesis testing to take place (revisit Test the Hypothesis, page 51).

Get Some Exposure

I wholeheartedly believe that exposing yourself to what you find frightening or panic-inducing gets you the most bang for your buck when overcoming panic attacks. Exposure (literally exposing yourself to a scary situation) is the most direct way to eliminate problematic avoidance behaviors. The challenge, of course, is that you have to be willing to put yourself in the situation that's triggering the fear of having another panic attack. So why on earth would you want to do that?

To reduce panic and anxiety, you need new experiences that teach your brain that panic attacks are not dangerous and life-threatening, and that the situations that might evoke panic attacks are also not dangerous and life-threatening. For this strategy to work, you need to do two things: First, you must actually face the fear and go to the situation that you are fearful of having a panic attack in. Second, you must not engage in any escape or avoidance behaviors, either mentally or physically. In other words, when exposing yourself to a trigger, the most effective thing you can do is stay present and open to whatever you are thinking and feeling, without trying to escape it or control it. Sitting with it and breathing are fine because you are staying in the moment with the panic, letting it wash over your body like a giant wave.

This strategy may sound scary at first, but the more you do it, the easier it gets. Why? Because every time you do it, you are reinforcing a new experience that says, "Hey, I got through this, and I am okay. I didn't die, I didn't have a heart attack, and I didn't go crazy. It was extremely uncomfortable, but I managed. And look, now things are feeling a little calmer and better again."

A crucial component for exposure to work is acceptance of the feelings, thoughts, and sensations that occur. There is no way to expose yourself to your panic attacks and panic-inducing situations without feeling some discomfort. So, my question to you is, will you embrace a certain amount of discomfort on your journey to a greater goal (in this case, reducing or limiting panic attacks)? Is it worth it to you to take back control of your life, even if it means facing more fear and discomfort in the short term? Do you value courage and taking on challenges to go after the things you want in your life that may have been limited by panic, like relationships, jobs, friends, and adventures?

By now I hope the answer to all of these questions is yes. If not, then exposure may not be the right approach at this time. If you would like to try to generate more willingness and motivation to take on the challenge of facing panic, then you might benefit from reflecting on your values, which you identified in chapter 1. If panic is disrupting or limiting any realms of your life (as it often does), then is that motivation enough for you to try something different? If you are motivated, but it feels too scary, then hopefully you can implement some of these strategies to start taking small steps forward to gain confidence. You can also work with a therapist who can help you deal with these fears and design the best game plan for you. (There's more on this in chapter 5; see Finding a Therapist, page 97.)

The main steps for effective exposure are creating a hierarchy (a blueprint for your exposure plan), identifying your common avoidance and escape behaviors, committing to a schedule of exposure exercises, following through on the exposures (starting with the easier ones and repeating them until they become much less anxiety-provoking and working your way up), and eliminating the avoidance behaviors. Getting motivated for the process helps, too.

CREATE A HIERARCHY

This hierarchy is a blueprint for your exposure plan. It gives you a concrete outline for what situations you feel the most anxiety about when it comes to your panic disorder. (You'll need your notebook or device for this exercise.) Begin by listing different situations and activities that induce panic or some lesser degree of anxiety.

Be sure to include many realistic activities and real-world situations that are impacting you. Just because you write something down doesn't mean you have to experience it. And don't worry about putting them in order yet; that part comes next. It's a good idea to get as many ideas out as you can right now; you can always edit them later. Here are just a few items that might appear on someone's list:

- Speaking up at the town hall meeting

- Going on a first date

- Meeting up with friends after work

- Attending a holiday party

- Driving a long distance

- Going on a job interview

- Filling my car up with gas

- Flying on an airplane

Once you have your list, rank each item on a scale of 1 to 10 with 10 being the most anxiety- or panic-inducing and 1 being relatively easy. Now reorder your list from most difficult to easiest. If you've given one or a few the same rank, just pick which one to list before the other.

Reflect on how you feel as you look at your list. Are you excited to expose yourself to any of these situations? Fearful or overwhelmed? These are normal reactions, so congratulate yourself for hanging in there and creating the hierarchy.

IDENTIFY WHAT YOU MIGHT DO TO AVOID OR ESCAPE

Look again at the hierarchy you just created in the previous strategy and determine how you would normally avoid or try to escape the things you listed. For example, if you usually convince yourself that you have to work late in order to not meet up with friends after work, you know that working late is a behavior you'll want to change so that you can start to get some exposure. If you do go to happy hour, do you spend a lot of time in the bathroom to escape your discomfort? You'll want to change this behavior, as well. If you avoid using your car and walk to the store even though it's several miles away because "Hey, exercise is good for me," when really you just want to avoid filling up your gas tank, you'll want to forgo that long walk for the time being.

Consider each item on your list and be sure to include all the ways you would normally try to avoid or escape those situations. If you can anticipate your likely avoidance and escape behaviors, you will be one step closer to eliminating them and sticking with your plan to expose yourself to the situation.

GET MOTIVATED

Looking again at your hierarchy, bring to mind all the benefits you will experience if you expose yourself to those panic-inducing situations and come out all the better for it. For example, if you speak up at the town hall meeting about a serious concern you have about your community, your voice will be heard and you can possibly further your agenda. If you drive a long distance or take a flight, you can visit a friend or relative you haven't seen in a while. Find motivation in the potential positive outcomes of exposing yourself to the situations you've listed. Also, revisit your values. What are the things worth taking a step forward for to bring you closer to what you value?

On the topic of motivation, you can also get inspired by watching other people exposing themselves to fearful situations. This activity can also help you reduce any nervousness you feel around the process. In the Resources section (page 105), I've listed some suggested videos to watch. Keep in mind that if you search the internet for more on exposure, you may come across some misinformation and naysayers, as is true for most things online. Some people may claim that exposure therapy doesn't work or you shouldn't do it because it's too scary. My response to that is, exposure may not be for everyone, but that doesn't mean the process is dangerous or faulty.

TRY IMAGINAL EXPOSURE

Imaginal exposure involves imagining yourself in the situation you've been avoiding. Of course you want to expose yourself to as many situations as possible, but sometimes you can't right away, if at all. For example, if a panic-inducing situation is speaking to an audience of thousands but it's likely you'll never face such a large audience, you can still imagine what it would feel like. Or if you avoid flying due to panic and you don't have any trips scheduled, you can still imagine yourself on the plane. You can also imagine yourself in situations that are feasible but you may not be ready to face yet. What's more, you can also use this strategy for the experience of an actual panic attack.

Imaginal exposure helps you connect with the fearful thoughts and feelings that might be running through your mind during the situation. Have your notebook and a recording device handy. Here are the steps for successful imaginal exposure:

1. Choose an item on your hierarchy. Think through that panic-inducing event from beginning to end, seeing yourself arriving, doing whatever it is you'd do in that situation, and so on.

2. Write a brief story about it in the present tense, including details of what you are thinking, feeling, and doing, and then record yourself reading this story.

3. Now, close your eyes and listen to your recording. The goal is to get your mind to believe that you are really in that difficult situation and having to face it.

Our minds are pretty good at mistaking imagined thoughts for reality (remember some of your cognitive distortions during a panic attack), which you can take advantage of to get some good exposure without even having to leave your living room.

GET OUT AND DO IT

Exposure can be scary and hard! Exposure therapy was originally designed to be done gradually, over time, and with a therapist. Starting with easier items on your hierarchy will help you build confidence and avoid becoming completely overwhelmed, which could lead you to become discouraged and disengage from the process. Commit to a reasonable schedule for tackling your hierarchy, repeat the steps until they become monotonous and almost habitual, and have fun with it!

Is it possible to just dive in and go for the hardest thing first? Yes. But few people will find this approach effective, so don't stress over the most difficult things on your list. If you have the option, you'll find that working with a trusted, knowledgeable professional on exposure therapy has enormous benefits. If not, you can turn to a trusted friend or family member for support, someone you can talk with and debrief after an exposure. Remember, it's okay to ask for help, and it's okay to have people with you when you are facing difficult situations. Support systems are great and help distribute the heavy load of taking on panic.

Now pick an item on your list that you know you can do. The difficulty level is not important right now. The most important thing is to pick something you will follow through with so that you start this process on the right foot. Commit to a time and place to complete your exposure (the sooner the better), and then get out and do it! Expose yourself to other situations on your list one by one to keep taking steps forward.

REFLECTION

Reflect on your exposure experience. How did it go? How did it feel? On a scale of 1 to 10, what was your panic and anxiety level? Did you experience a full-blown panic attack? Did you expect that you would have a panic attack beforehand? Which physical symptoms were the worst and how did you handle them? What thoughts came to mind, and were you able to reframe them? What avoidance or escape behavior did you conquer? Are you willing to practice exposure again to get the life you want? Think about these questions and write down your observations.

Go Deeper: Interoceptive Exposure

A unique form of exposure for panic attacks is called interoceptive exposure. Interoceptive exposure means exposing yourself to all the physiological symptoms of a panic attack. So, instead of just going to the situation that creates a panic attack and doing your best, the idea here is to break down your panic attack into the actual physical sensations that feel the scariest and worst to you and to tackle them independently.

The goal is to have a new experience that teaches you "heart racing = not scary" or "dizzy, lightheaded feeling = not a problem." Repetition is key for lowering your anxiety in response to the physical discomfort you are going to feel. Take a moment to remember some of your cognitive reframes. Your heart races when you exercise, but you generally don't freak out when that happens. Similarly, donating blood or standing up too fast can cause a lightheaded feeling but doesn't always lead to panic attacks. You are training your brain to see that the same physical sensations of panic attacks are not necessarily dangerous. And once you have that understanding, what else is a panic attack besides a bunch of false predictions and unpleasant physical sensations?

There are eight primary exercises you can do to expose yourself to the most common unpleasant panic attack symptoms. If you are going to try interoceptive exposure, I suggest picking one or two exercises first. Then, as you gain confidence, you can start doing more and combining them. For each activity, rate the level of physical intensity on a scale of 1 to 10, with 10 being most intense, and rate your anxiety level on a scale of 1 to 10, with 10 being most anxious.

>

The goal is for you to engage so intensely that you get the physical intensity to at least an 8. Again, first and foremost, do not do anything that might put you in danger. But if you think you are ready, this strategy will go a long way to reducing your fear of panic attacks. These exercises can also be done with a therapist or trusted person if you are unsure about any of them.

1. Hold your breath until it feels like you really can't anymore (diaphragm spasms).

2. Breathe through a straw, constricting your airflow (mimicking the feeling of suffocating).

3. Spin in a chair for 20 seconds (dizziness).

4. Do jumping jacks or run upstairs (heart racing).

5. Stand in front of a mirror and stare into your eyes without moving your gaze for two minutes (may elicit feelings of derealization or depersonalization; feeling "out of it").

6. Hang your head down in front of you while seated for one minute, then stand up quickly (head rush or lightheaded feeling).

7. Intentionally hyperventilate for 30 to 45 seconds. This can be scary, but it's not dangerous.

8. Tense all the muscles in your body and hold for one minute (shaking or muscle tension).

Again, work on these interoceptive exposure exercises only when you feel ready to tackle them.

TAKEAWAYS

- Avoidance makes panic and anxiety worse, even though it feels calming in the moment.

- Acceptance, distraction, mindfulness, breathing, and sitting with the feelings are all practical alternatives to avoidance.

- Exposure to the thoughts, feelings, sensations, and situations that induce panic is your most effective tool for overcoming panic.

- You can start building your confidence by taking on easier exposure challenges first and working your way up.

Chapter 5

Looking Ahead

I hope you now have a better understanding of how panic attacks affect your body, mind, and behavior. The strategies throughout this book are a good jumping-off point for tackling this difficult issue. This final chapter reinforces the concepts discussed, encourages you to stick with a plan that works for you to overcome your panic and anxiety, and offers some suggestions for where to go from here. The take-home message here is practice, practice, practice. To get the result you want, you will need to be patient and consistent and put in the time. Overcoming panic is a marathon, not a sprint. Make a plan, set several reminders to help you, and stick to it. If you find yourself struggling and need additional support and help (as we all sometimes do!), please ask for it, whether by seeking professional counseling, looking for a group or online resource, or talking to a trusted friend or family member.

Long-Term Outlook

Congratulations on getting this far in your journey to overcome anxiety and panic! If you have been practicing the strategies, I commend you for all your work, courage, and determination. Chances are you've already started to see the benefits and progress in the form of reduced panic symptoms and fewer attacks. Perhaps you are noticing a decrease in intensity of the physiological symptoms or an increased ability to tolerate them. You might also start to see that some situations you had previously been avoiding are getting a little bit easier to manage. If so, keep up the good work! Panic attacks may crop up in the future, even after periods of minimal anxiety. There will be potentially triggering situations throughout your life as you grow and take on new challenges and experiences. However, the more you remember to use the strategies that work best for you and openly approach and accept your feelings, the more flexible and richer your life will be.

If you haven't noticed as much progress as you would like, don't be discouraged. Overcoming panic is hard work! I have spent my career studying and working with this issue, and I still need help from time to time. Panic and anxiety are not things that live inside us that we can just cut out. They are more like aches and pains that need different strategies to be cared for and healed. There is no one-size-fits-all approach, which is why I've provided a good variety of strategies you can use to manage panic attacks in your life.

Will they go away entirely? Probably not. But that outcome doesn't have to be the goal. A more realistic goal is to use these strategies to increase flexibility in your life so that you can move toward your values and the experiences that matter to you most without being held back by fear. Remember, fear is a natural response to many challenging, new, and meaningful situations, so don't get down on yourself for experiencing panic and anxiety. Keep those thoughts, feelings, and physical sensations in perspective, and you will see that you are much more resilient than your panic attacks would have you believe.

You can practice several of the strategies in this book (such as mindfulness and progressive muscle relaxation) every day to maximize their effectiveness as a buffer before or during a panic attack. Certain strategies (such as exposure, acceptance, and cognitive reframing) will provide the most benefit when you can practice them during a panic attack to mitigate the intensity of the experience and develop confidence in your ability to handle the situation. I realize that it takes time to get to this point. However, there is just no shortcut for exposure. I understand this process can be scary, and I commend you for taking on the challenge. So remember, by using these tools, you can face your fears and ultimately overcome them.

Your Biggest Victories So Far

Mindfully and intentionally reflecting on your victories is a good way to reinforce positive behaviors, because sometimes our minds have a tendency to overlook the positives and focus on the negatives (remember the cognitive distortion called filtering, described on page 48). Reflect back on your journey so far and identify some of your victories, no matter how small or insignificant they may feel. A seemingly small victory may be your biggest. For example, if you've been consistently practicing a strategy and it is starting to get a little easier, that's something to celebrate. Maybe you have gotten really good at a particular strategy and you want to start working on another. Good for you! Are you catching cognitive distortions when they come up and responding to them differently? Are you more tolerant of the physical sensations of panic now? Consider these questions and more to identify your victories.

By engaging in a behavior that may elicit some panic or anxiety, you are teaching yourself that you are in the driver's seat of your life and you are willing to take on whatever may come. Getting out of your comfort zone and facing previously avoided situations, people, or events is a huge step in your progress, so please pause and give yourself some credit. Now is a great time to treat yourself as a reward for the work you have put in.

Your Biggest Challenges So Far

I know that facing panic attacks is not all sunshine and rainbows. Take a moment here to honestly check in on your biggest challenges in this process. The point is not to beat yourself up emotionally but rather to accept the reality of the situation and approach thinking about things that are difficult, painful, or scary. In doing so, you are taking another step toward being able to do something about it. Even if it feels like panic attacks are still running your life and leading to avoidance of a lot of important things, that's okay. The good news is there are more options available to you beyond this book if you need additional help, such as individual therapy, group therapy, and online resources, which I'll discuss in Building Your Support Network (page 96). So, be honest with yourself and take a minute to reflect on your biggest challenges.

Maybe you've been procrastinating or forgetting to work on the strategies. That's something within your power to change. Maybe you are finding certain strategies too difficult or don't really understand how they could work in the midst of a panic attack. Perhaps you are having trouble reframing your thoughts and keep getting stuck on a certain one. Is your fear of certain physiological symptoms limiting your ability to face challenging situations? Consider these points and more so that you can figure out what your next steps are.

Go Deeper: Targeting Your Biggest Challenges with Goal Setting

When you know what your biggest challenges are, you can choose one to work through by setting a goal for yourself. The phrase "keep it short and simple"—otherwise known as KISS—can help you remember to break down challenging goals into smaller, more attainable steps. Taking smaller steps toward your long-term goal can help you stay on track and motivated by your progress. Maybe your long-term goal is to be able to socialize at a party without trying to "escape" early due to worries about having a panic attack. Smaller goals might include engaging in small talk with a few people during a lunch date and practicing reframing your panicky thoughts. In this way, short-term goals can eventually lead to your long-term goal.

An important element of goal setting is to make your goals positive, observable behaviors. An easy test is to ask yourself, "Could a person who is asleep accomplish this goal just as easily as I can?" If so, it's not a great goal. For example, the goal "Don't freak out at the party" is not helping you accomplish anything, so it's not a productive goal. A better goal would be "Say hello to two people at the party."

Another concept around goal setting is to not set goals that are based on thoughts and feelings. For example, a goal might be to go to the museum and not feel embarrassed. This goal is not useful because, at this stage, you have little control over the thoughts and feelings you might experience at the museum. And, in fact, if going to the museum is on your hierarchy for exposure, you would expect to feel some anxiety about going and being there. A more helpful short-term goal in this case would perhaps be to take a child you know to a children's museum and make eye contact with five people there, or plan to spend just a half hour at a smaller museum and say hi to one person. >

In your notebook or device, break down your biggest challenges into smaller steps, which you can then tackle one at a time, maybe with the support of another person, until the smaller steps feel more manageable and you're in a good position to tackle your next short-term goal.

The Road to Progress Isn't Always Straight

Overcoming your fear around panic attacks is not a straightforward process like learning a foreign language or a musical instrument. Generally, there isn't too much regression in the learning process, and the more you practice, the more you continue to build your skills. Conversely, learning to overcome panic is not so linear. There will be days when you feel more confident, and certain situations will be tackled with ease. The next week, the same situation might cue up some of those old thoughts and feelings. Remember, progress in this area may involve setbacks, so don't get down on yourself when they occur.

A key to your overall progress is recognizing that it isn't measured by the presence or absence of your panic and anxiety symptoms. Yes, the goal is to ultimately experience less anxiety and panic, but if there is one thing I want you to take away from this book, it is the idea that how you *respond* to panic and anxiety is up to you. Your willingness to respond with courage and openness, consistent with your values, is a better measure of progress. Like many things in life that are challenging, overcoming anxiety takes work. If it were easy, you'd already be doing it, so of course there are going to be some bumps along the way. However, I can think of few challenges that are more worthwhile than facing your anxiety and panic. This is your life! What could be more important?

Be wary that your mind may have tried to convince you that the things you are avoiding, and therefore missing in your life, really aren't that important. Do not give in to this distortion. Avoidance and stories like "It's too much work," "I can't do it," or "It will never work out anyway" are part of the trap you must not let yourself fall into. You hold the keys to your own future success, not panic! Those stories have less hold on you when your strategies become second nature, and because this is a process, it's important to track your progress on a daily, weekly, and monthly basis to keep your mind focused on the work you are doing. Tracking your progress also highlights your victories. We all get a little kick of that feel-good chemical dopamine when we accomplish something, so take advantage of it and give yourself small goals to check off regularly.

Scheduling regular check-ins with yourself is also important. It's natural to stop being so diligent when you start to feel better and believe panic and anxiety are less of a problem for you. However, by regularly checking in with your goals and progress, or setting reminders to review this book and notes you've taken, you can keep the momentum going, prevent relapses, and decrease the chances of panic attacks showing up at inopportune times in the future.

Build Your New Habits

Remember, change does not happen overnight. Like many things worth doing in life, the real benefits show up after much time and effort. When the strategies you've learned become habits and the concepts are a more natural part of your mindset, you'll start to notice that life is taking you in the direction you want to go. However, before something becomes a habit, intentional practice is necessary. Committing to tracking your behavior on a daily basis keeps you focused on the work you are doing to reduce the severity and frequency of your panic attacks and anxiety. Remaining focused on this work is a necessary step toward turning your new behaviors and approaches into second-nature behaviors and can keep you from getting caught in avoidance traps and cognitive distortions that stop you from just doing it.

TRACK YOUR BEHAVIOR DAILY

If you haven't been taking notes throughout this book, it is time to decide how you will track your behavior on a daily basis. You can use a notebook or a notes app on your mobile device—whatever works for you and will give you the highest likelihood of following through. Pick a time, perhaps after dinner or as part of your bedtime routine, to spend a few minutes taking notes on each of the following:

- Avoidance or escape behaviors you used throughout the day

- Exposure exercises you tried

- Cognitive distortions and reframes you used

- General healthy habits—sleep, physical activity, eating well, mindfulness exercises, and so on

A sample entry might look like this:

I avoided asking a question at work even though I was confused. I completed my exposure exercise of saying good morning to three coworkers. I caught myself catastrophizing about having a panic attack at the doctor's office and I did a quick reframe, reminding myself that I can survive a panic attack if I have one. I ate a serving of vegetables today and did a body scan.

Give yourself credit for all your accomplishments every day. On the days when you don't see much progress, be kind to yourself and pick one item to take on the next day so you don't get caught up in the negative.

DON'T WAIT FOR YOUR MIND TO BE READY

The statement "Just do it!" seems so simple, but it can be very difficult to follow through on. However, it's a theme I can't emphasize enough. When facing panic and anxiety, it is tempting to get caught in a battle with your mind, trying to convince yourself not to be anxious or panic. As discussed in chapter 3, there are so many ways to get trapped in cognitive distortions that it's better to just commit to an action—whether or not your mind is ready. In fact, it is unlikely you will ever truly "feel ready" to take on something uncomfortable. As such, don't wait around for confirmation from your mind that it's the right time. Don't overthink it. Just pick an action item and do it.

Let's say it's Monday and you are invited to a lecture Friday evening at the library on a topic of interest. You initially say yes, but as Friday afternoon approaches, you start to feel your anxiety building and your mind starts worrying about what will happen if you have a panic attack at the library. You are tempted to tell your friend you're worn out from the week. But you don't. You don't bargain with your mind or try to convince yourself not to be anxious. You accept those feelings and you go to the lecture. Maybe panic shows up; maybe it doesn't. Either way, you did it, and you feel more confident that you can get through the next challenge.

Checkups and Check-Ins

In life, we all need regular "checkups" to keep things running smoothly, and overcoming anxiety and panic is no different. Our cars need an oil change from time to time, the tires in our bikes need to be filled, our homes have to be maintained, we need to go in for regular physicals and dental visits, and so on. Many of these things are prescheduled. So, in your process of learning to deal with panic attacks, you will need to schedule regular checkups for yourself to keep your mental health running smoothly, as well.

When you check in with yourself at these scheduled checkups, you'll have an opportunity to reflect on how you are doing in your journey of overcoming panic. You can pull out this book, look over your tracking logs, talk with a therapist or friend, or journal about your experience so far. These are all effective ways of keeping you from falling back into old patterns. Furthermore, if you keep these strategies at the forefront of your mind, then they will be more effective when you run into a new, challenging situation that does elicit some anxiety and panicky feelings. And, when you successfully navigate challenging situations, the positive momentum builds on itself, leading to more confidence and fewer panic attacks moving forward. Your life will continue to expand and broaden, leading to more meaningful and enriching experiences.

SET INTERMITTENT REMINDERS

If you have a smartphone that you check regularly, take advantage of it by setting up several reminders on a few random days to remind you to practice your strategies. Aim for about five a month. You can set reminders on your computer or tablet, as well, or even through a virtual assistant, like Amazon's Alexa or Apple's Siri. If you don't use electronic devices, you can make notes in a daily planner or calendar. Then, if you've gotten distracted or complacent in your process, when this reminder pops up, it can help you get back on track.

What should these reminders be? A variety of things. For each reminder, pick a different concept, including mindfulness, acceptance, exposure, or cognitive restructuring. You can simply have a word pop up (for example, "mindfulness"), or you can ask a question, such as "How are you doing with acceptance?" You can also remind yourself to practice an exercise you like or a strategy you find difficult or to do something outside your comfort zone. The intermittent reminders will help keep you practicing until the strategies become regular habits.

THREE-MONTH REMINDER

Set a reminder for three months from now on either your electronic device or your paper calendar. When this day arrives, it's time to revisit this book and review all the notes you've taken. Also, reflect on the following questions:

- What have I given up in my life because of panic? Check back in with your values if you need a reminder.

- Have I gotten those things back? If so, how does that feel? If not, what have I been avoiding?

- Do I need more help or do I need to practice the strategies again? If so, which strategies?

This book is meant to be an active companion on your journey, so this three-month reminder will help you return to it, if needed. This journey is challenging and it will take a sustained effort over time to get the maximum benefit.

Go Deeper: Weekly Strategies Calendar

Overcoming panic attacks requires patience and consistency. Practicing these strategies regularly will help turn them into habits, making them more effective at reducing the intensity of panic in the moment and the likelihood of panic in the first place. Put the following plan into place ahead of time when you are feeling fine, so that it's ready to go when you are feeling stressed, strained, and/or tired.

1. Get out a paper calendar or use the one on your phone, tablet, or computer.

2. Pick a day to start each new week. I suggest Sunday, because most people have this day off from work and view it as the beginning or end of the week.

>

3. Pick one new strategy for each week for the next five weeks. If you're feeling ambitious, pick two or three, but don't overwhelm yourself.

4. Now write them down in your calendar or planner on each of the next five Sundays. You can abbreviate them so that you know what your note is referring to when you see it.

If you need to, make a copy of, transcribe, or bookmark the particular strategy so that you can refer back to it easily when the day comes.

The purpose is to remove forgetfulness and procrastination as excuses and reasons for not following up on your exercises and check-ins. It's in the calendar so you don't have to think about it. Just engage like you would when showing up to a meeting, going to a doctor's appointment, or picking your kid up from soccer practice. Remember to bring openness, honesty, and compassion with you when you engage in an exercise or practice a strategy.

Building Your Support Network

To paraphrase the Beatles, things are better with a little help from your friends. It's a good idea to get support from friends, family, a therapist, group therapy, online support, or coworkers when you're overcoming emotional difficulties, including panic attacks. Humans are social beings by nature, and we rely on one another to get through hard times. The challenge here is that social interaction might be one of your cues for panic attacks, so what then? In that case, it is important to lean into this feeling (that is, feel it fully) and do some deeper investigating to see if *everyone* in your life really cues up intense anxiety, or if there are some people in certain situations with whom you feel a little safer and easier. If there are, they are the people you'll want to open up to and talk to a little bit about your experience.

Even if not everyone has panic attacks, anxiety is a universal human experience. You might even find that you actually feel closer with people when you share your experience of anxiety, as they will often respond with support, validation, and understanding. Taking the risk of being vulnerable enhances connection with others and can make you feel more normal and less crazy in the process.

Regarding professional help, we live in a time when there is a wealth of services available for mental health. The stigmatization of anxiety disorders and other mental health issues continues to decrease every year as we as a society accept and acknowledge the actual suffering that has long been taking place in this country. Many insurance plans now offer counseling benefits, and there are clinics throughout the country that offer low-cost therapy services for people with low income or who are on Medicaid. In addition to traditional, individual therapy, people suffering from anxiety and panic attacks can often find support and relief in group therapy. Group therapy is typically a lower-cost alternative where you learn the same skills as individual therapy and get the benefit of immediate validation and support from people who have similar experiences. Another alternative to in-person counseling is online support and virtual therapy. Whatever your preference is, you don't need to struggle alone.

Finding a Therapist

There are a few good options for finding a therapist in your area. A quick way is to search the internet and visit reputable sites, such as PsychologyToday.com, to find a therapist in your area. There are also other online therapist directories, including GoodTherapy.org and OpenPathCollective.org, which has a directory of clinicians offering low-cost services. (You'll find a few more recommendations in the Resources section, page 105.) You could also go through your insurance, either online or by calling, to find in-network therapists who specialize in anxiety/panic disorder. Therapy can be expensive, so find out the costs up front, and explore a variety of options to find something that works for you.

Therapists utilize many different approaches to treating anxiety and panic. I highly recommend finding a therapist who will challenge you to confront panic attacks, preferably using exposure with response prevention (that's just the formal name for exposure therapy; *response prevention* refers to the process of blocking your avoidance/escape behaviors to make the exposure maximally effective). These therapists usually practice CBT and ACT, and in the Resources section (page 105), you'll find a few suggested sites to visit. Find a few names, call them up, and ask them specifically what methods they use to treat panic attacks. Remember to ask them questions about exposure or avoidance and share a little bit about what you are experiencing. This vetting process is the best way to get a feel for your fit with the therapist, which is going to predict how effective the therapy is. I encourage you to be thoughtful in this process and not rush it.

Support Groups

Support groups are becoming increasingly popular. Group therapy is a great way to force yourself to face your fears and take on the challenges of panic attacks while getting the support you need from others who know exactly what you are experiencing. Support groups can provide genuine empathy and advice from people who know what it's like to live with the fear of panic attacks lurking in the back of their minds. They will often have useful suggestions for what worked for them, and groups can help hold you accountable to the goals you set for yourself.

You can find groups in your area by searching on sites like Meetup.com and PsychologyToday.com. You can also use your internet browser to find groups in your area with keywords such as "support groups near me." An online search is the fastest method, but you can also call or email individual therapists who work with panic and anxiety and ask them if they know of any anxiety- or panic-specific groups nearby. Other places to inquire about groups are churches, community mental health centers, school counseling centers, and doctors' offices.

Therapy and support groups are typically more affordable than individual counseling and sometimes meet less frequently, so you won't feel overwhelmed making a big time commitment is a concern for you. You can usually try out the group once or twice, or at least meet with the group leaders first, before making a formal commitment. Again, be sure to talk to the leaders ahead of time, and ask questions about what models and methods they ascribe to and how they can be helpful to you. You might also find that the groups are a good way to make new friends.

Online Support

Although the internet can provide a wealth of supportive resources to those suffering from panic attacks, be careful when sifting through bad or unhelpful information; generally the more knowledge you have on the topic, the better. Not only is information helpful in getting a leg up on your panic attacks, but engaging in online support groups, chats, and discussion boards and forums can make you feel a lot more normal when things feel so out of control. Millions of Americans suffer from panic attacks, and you can connect with these people without having to leave your home or meet anyone new. You can find online support groups, chats, and forums on sites such as Reddit, Google Groups (groups.google.com), and Facebook.

Additionally, there are now more resources available to offer online text and chat support from a therapist. Check out BetterHelp.com, Teledoc.com, and Talkspace.com. These can be live interactions by video chat, or you can exchange messages throughout the day or week depending on what you need. I like this option because these companies are reducing barriers to helping people get some form of treatment. And you will often find that just knowing at least one person out there is listening can help you make sense of an issue, clarify your goals, and take the first steps. A lot of people may not have the time, money, or means to physically go to a therapist's office to work on their panic attacks, or they don't want anyone to find out about their visits to a therapist. Whatever the reason, these online resources can be a valuable alternative to help you evaluate your own treatment needs with another person and see what works for you.

Many people find that therapy (and the therapeutic strategies discussed in this book), prescription medication, or a combination of both is helpful in overcoming their panic attacks. Research indicates and supports that medication is effective in the treatment of panic attacks. If you decide that you would like to explore this option, consult your primary care doctor or a psychiatrist. Although many primary care doctors are more accessible and willing to prescribe medications for treating panic attacks, they have less specialized knowledge in the treatment of mental health issues in general, given that they are responsible for treating medical issues of all types. Therefore, I recommend that you try to make an appointment with a psychiatrist or psychiatric nurse so you can get more detailed information and specific advice related to your panic attacks and any other mental health concerns you may have. I understand that psychiatrists can be expensive, may not be covered by insurance, or can have long waiting lists, so you have to do whatever makes the most sense for you given these factors. I encourage you to do your own research and speak to a doctor if you feel medication would complement the work you are doing in this book and/or with your therapist.

Staying the Course

You've learned the tools, you've set your goals, you have a plan to execute them, and you've identified where you might slip up and avoid. However, maybe when the day comes to follow through on your plan, the panicky feeling shows up, you revert to your old ways, and you feel defeated. I've seen this scenario time and again with clients, and I know it from personal experience, as well. It's a terrible feeling because we know we are capable of so much more. So, how can you help keep yourself accountable to follow through with practicing strategies and achieving your goals? Here are two final strategies to help you continue to heal from panic.

MAKE A COMMITMENT TO YOURSELF

Declare to yourself right now that overcoming panic attacks is important to you. You're clearly sick of suffering and feeling this way or you wouldn't have picked up this book in the first place. Make a commitment right here, right now, that when it gets hard (and it *will* get hard), you will come back to this book, your goals, your values, and your hopes for a better life, and you will not be dominated by panic and fear; instead, you will lean into the discomfort and forge ahead.

Use your notebook or device and write your commitment to yourself in one or two sentences. Use strong, assertive language. Here's an example:

I hereby commit to sticking to my plan and goals, using these strategies to overcome panic, so that I can be freer in my life, especially at work and in my relationships.

SET YOURSELF UP FOR SUCCESS

Be sure to set yourself up for success with regular reminders, support, and practice. Use the ideas provided in this book to help keep you afloat. In addition to setting reminders and scheduling check-ins, some creative ideas to nudge yourself to practice your strategies and do the work include leaving yourself sticky notes on your mirrors and throughout your house, talking with your friends and family, or enlisting the help of a therapist or support group. Don't take on all the difficulty alone! Keep this book by your bedside until you have started making real progress so that it is in easy arm's reach and you can look at it every day.

Mark things off on your checklist, calendar, or exposure hierarchy every time you accomplish something, so that you are giving yourself the acknowledgment and praise you deserve for your effort. Trust in the process and trust in yourself, and the rest will follow.

TAKEAWAYS

- Practice the strategies discussed in this book over and over again until they become habits.

- Set small, realistic goals so that you start to see some progress immediately and can hold yourself accountable to staying on track.

- Build your support network and enlist the help of friends, family, or professionals to assist you. Challenges are easier when you have someone by your side.

RESOURCES

Therapist Directories

Association for Behavioral and Cognitive Therapies
http://www.abct.org/Home/
This organization's website has lots of great information on CBT, including articles, resources, and videos to give you more in-depth knowledge about CBT interventions.

Directory of CBT Therapists
http://www.findcbt.org/FAT/
The Association for Behavioral and Cognitive Therapies directory lists therapists across the country who ascribe to the CBT model of therapy.

Association for Contextual Behavioral Science
https://contextualscience.org/
This comprehensive website contains ACT principles, resources, research articles, and a directory of ACT therapists.

Psychology Today
https://www.psychologytoday.com/us
Psychology Today has a comprehensive therapist directory with listings from therapists across all disciplines, locations, insurances, and education and training levels.

Books

Get Out of Your Mind and Into Your Life: The New Acceptance and Commitment Therapy by Steven C. Hayes, PhD, with Spencer Smith
This resource is the original ACT workbook for tackling any mental health issue and is very applicable to your journey to overcoming panic attacks, as it provides many useful exercises and strategies helping you face your fears.

The Confidence Gap: A Guide to Overcoming Fear and Self-Doubt by Russ Harris
This book is probably my favorite easy read on anxiety, with lots of relatable examples, strategies, and tools for tackling anxiety.

Things Might Go Terribly, Horribly, Wrong: A Guide to Life Liberated from Anxiety by Kelly G. Wilson, PhD, and Troy DuFrene
Wilson is one of the founders of ACT and focuses on acceptance and mindfulness interventions for anxiety in this book.

TED Talks

"The Power of Vulnerability" by Brené Brown
https://bit.ly/33tYdJP
This talk is a must-watch for anyone with anxiety, self-confidence issues, panic attacks, self-esteem issues, or relationship difficulties. Dr. Brown is a powerful, engaging speaker who communicates her message with compassion and grace.

Articles

American Psychological Association, "What Is Exposure Therapy?"
apa.org/ptsd-guideline/patients-and-families/exposure-therapy
This quick read is for anyone who wants to learn a little bit more about what exposure therapy is and how it can be useful.

Psychiatric Times, "Exposure Therapy for Anxiety Disorders" by
Johanna S. Kaplan, PhD, and David F. Tolin, PhD
https://www.psychiatrictimes.com/anxiety/exposure-therap
y-anxiety-disorders
This article helps explain more about the effectiveness of exposure
therapy with anxiety disorders specifically.

Exposure Therapy Videos

"Exposure to Suffocation Fears" by Reid Wilson, PhD
https://bit.ly/2Qt1JPx
In this quick, five-minute video of a therapy session, the client
engages in an exposure therapy exercise related to panic attacks, in
this case, the fear of suffocating. It shows you that you can really
practice exposure and that it is effective.

**"Exposure Therapy Pushing Yourself to Get Better | Anxiety |
Agoraphobia"**
https://bit.ly/2xbC07l
This homemade video shows an average person with agoraphobia
(fear of having panic attacks when he leaves his home) engaging in
an exposure and talking through his thoughts and feelings during
the experience. It offers hope and encouragement to others who
are looking to tackle this issue.

Mindfulness and Meditation App

Headspace for iPhone and Android
headspace.com/headspace-meditation-app
Headspace is a free, easy-to-use app that teaches you the basics
of mindfulness and meditation and helps you track your progress
and commit to daily activities.

REFERENCES

Agarwal, Ulka, Suruchi Mishra, Jia Xu, Susan Levin, Joseph Gonzales, and Neal D. Barnard. "A Multicenter Randomized Controlled Trial of a Nutrition Intervention Program in a Multiethnic Adult Population in the Corporate Setting Reduces Depression and Anxiety and Improves Quality of Life: The GEICO Study." *American Journal of Health Promotion* 29, no. 4 (March 2015): 245–54. doi: 10.4278 /ajhp.130218-QUAN-72.

American Psychological Association. "Stress Effects on the Body." Accessed February 12, 2020. apa.org/topics/stress-body.

Anxiety and Depression Association of America. "Irritable Bowel Syndrome (IBS)." Accessed February 12, 2020. adaa.org/understanding-anxiety/related-illnesses /irritable-bowel-syndrome-ibs.

Asmundson, Gordon J. G., Mathew G. Fetzner, Lindsey B. DeBoer, Mark B. Powers, Michael W. Otto, and Jasper A. J. Smits. "Let's Get Physical: A Contemporary Review of the Anxiolytic Effects of Exercise for Anxiety and Its Disorders." *Depression and Anxiety* 30, no. 4 (April 2013): 362–73. doi: 10.1002/da.22043.

Clark, David A., and Aaron T. Beck. *Cognitive Therapy of Anxiety Disorders: Science and Practice.* New York: Guilford Press, 2010.

Cleveland Clinic. "Vital Signs." Accessed February 12, 2020. my.clevelandclinic.org /health/articles/10881-vital-signs.

Delmonte, M. M. "Meditation and Anxiety Reduction: A Literature Review." *Clinical Psychology Review* 5, no. 2 (1985): 91–102. Accessed February 16, 2020. doi: 10.1016/0272-7358(85)90016-9.

Eifler, Aleksandra. "The Interaction between Your Nervous System and Digestion." *Vita Infuse Yourself With Life* (blog). January 13, 2017. Accessed February 12, 2020. infuseyourself.life/your-nervous-system-digestion/.

Grohol, John M. "15 Common Cognitive Distortions." *PsychCentral*. Last updated June 24, 2019. psychcentral.com/lib/15-common-cognitive-distortions/.

Hayes, Steven C., Kirk D. Strosahl, and Kelly G. Wilson. *Acceptance and Commitment Therapy: The Process and Practice of Mindful Change.* New York: Guilford Press, 2012.

Hayes, Steven C., Michael E. Levin, Jennifer Plumb-Vilardaga, Jennifer L. Villatte, and Jacqueline Pistorello. "Acceptance and Commitment Therapy and Contextual Behavioral Science: Examining the Progress of a Distinctive Model of Behavioral and Cognitive Therapy." *Behavior Therapy* 44, no. 2 (June 2013): 180–98. doi: 10.1016/j.beth.2009.08.002.

Huffman, Jeff C., Mark H. Pollack, and Theodore A. Stern. "Panic Disorder and Chest Pain: Mechanisms, Morbidity, and Management." *Primary Care Companion to the Journal of Clinical Psychiatry* 4, no. 2 (March 2002): 54–62. doi: 10.4088/pcc. v04n0203.

Lardieri, Alexa. "Study: Meditation Improves Anxiety and Cardiovascular Health." *U.S. News & World Report*, April 20, 2018. usnews.com/news/health-care-news /articles/2018-04-20/study-meditation-improves-anxiety-and-cardiovascular -health.

Laskowski, Edward R. "What's a Normal Resting Heart Rate?" Mayo Clinic. August 29, 2018. mayoclinic.org/healthy-lifestyle/fitness/expert-answers /heart-rate/faq-20057979.

Medical News Today. "What Are Some Foods to Ease Your Anxiety?" Accessed February 12, 2020. medicalnewstoday.com/articles/322652.php.

Ratey, John J. "Can Exercise Help Treat Anxiety?" *Harvard Health Publishing* (blog). October 24, 2019. health.harvard.edu/blog/can-exercise-help-treat -anxiety-2019102418096.

Richter, Ruthann. "Among Teens, Sleep Deprivation an Epidemic." *Stanford Medicine News Center*. October 8, 2015. med.stanford.edu/news/all-news/2015/10/among -teens-sleep-deprivation-an-epidemic.html.

Sawchuk, Craig N. "Coping with Anxiety: Can Diet Make a Difference?" Mayo Clinic. May 24, 2017. mayoclinic.org/diseases-conditions/generalized-anxiety-disorder /expert-answers/coping-with-anxiety/faq-20057987.

Sheps, MD, Sheldon G. "Anxiety: A Cause of High Blood Pressure?" Mayo Clinic. March 4, 2020. mayoclinic.org/diseases-conditions/high-blood-pressure /expert-answers/anxiety/faq-20058549.

Tsuda, Akira, Masatoshi Tanaka, Tadashi Nishikawa, Hisashi Hirai, and William P. Paré. "Effects of Unpredictability versus Loss of Predictability of Shock on Gastric Lesions in Rats." *Physiological Psychology* 11 (December 1983): 287–90. doi: 10.3758/BF03326809.

INDEX

ACKNOWLEDGMENTS

Thanks to the editing team at Callisto Media for their hard work in helping develop this book. I also want to acknowledge my professors and supervisors who have helped me develop my knowledge and skills in working with individuals with panic and anxiety throughout my career. And thank you to my wife, my friends, and family, who help keep me grounded and push me to take on challenges, including writing this book. I am very lucky to have your support in my life.

ABOUT THE AUTHOR

David Shanley, PsyD, is a licensed psychologist in Denver, Colorado. He has personally struggled with different forms of anxiety throughout his life and utilized the strategies discussed to overcome these challenges. He now works in private practice helping adults with anxiety, OCD, PTSD, and panic attacks work through their issues and find flexibility and meaning in their lives. The process is not always easy, and it never looks the same for two different individuals. However, with persistence, patience, and willingness, Dr. Shanley has seen hundreds of clients successfully navigate their struggles with anxiety and panic. When not in the office, Dr. Shanley enjoys all of the outdoor activities that Colorado has to offer throughout the seasons. He is also the author of *The Social Anxiety Workbook for Work, Public & Social Life.* Visit DrDavidShanley.com.